BECOMING THE MANIFESTING DIVA

CREATING RIPPLES WHILE YOU FLOW

KATIE CAREY – AMMA VENTELÄ – DANIELLE DEMOSS
DIANE BOVALINO – GISELLE LORENA HURTADO
JO-ANNE ROSS – KARLA KOPP – KATIE GAUTHIER
LOUISE SAMOSORN – MARIE SCHLEMM
REVEREND STACEY PIEDRAHITA
DR. SUSANNE KURZ – YANA WELLER

FOREWORD BY DR. JOE VITALE

SOULFUL VALLEY PUBLISHING

Copyright © 2024 by Katie Carey of Soulful Valley Publishing
Edited by Angela Harders of PAX Ministries Publishing
Formatted by Katie Carey of Soulful Valley Publishing

All rights reserved. Apart from any fair dealing for the purposes of research, private study, criticism, or review, as permitted under the Copyright, Designs and Patents Act of 1988, this publication may only be reproduced, stored, or transmitted in any form or by any means with the prior permission in writing of the copyright owner, or in this case, of the reprographic reproduction in accordance with the terms of licensees issued by the Copyright Licensing Agency. Enquiries concerning reproduction outside those terms should be sent to the publisher.

Disclaimer

The publisher and the authors are providing this book on an "as is" basis and make no representations or warranties of any kind with respect to the book or its contents. The publisher and the authors disclaim all such representations and warranties of healthcare for a particular purpose. In addition, the publisher and the authors assume no responsibility for errors, inaccuracies, omissions, or any other consistencies herein.

The content of this book is for informational purposes only and is not intended to diagnose, treat, cure, or prevent any condition or disease. You understand that this book is not intended as a substitute for consultation with a licensed practitioner. Please consult with your own physician or healthcare specialist regarding the suggestions and recommendations made in this book. The use of this book implies your acceptance of this disclaimer.

The publisher and the authors make no guarantees concerning the level of success you may experience by following the advice and strategies contained in this book, and you accept the risk that results will differ for each individual. The testimonials and examples provided in this book show exceptional results which may not apply to the average reader and are not intended to represent or guarantee that you will achieve the same or similar results.

This is a work of creative nonfiction. The events portrayed have been done so to the best of each author's memory. While all the stories in this book are true, some names and identifying details have been changed to protect the privacy of the people involved.

FOREWORD

Invitation to Your Miracle

Welcome, dear reader, to a journey of empowerment, transformation, and manifestation. I'm thrilled to introduce you to "Becoming the Manifesting Diva: Creating Ripples While You Flow," a collaborative book that brings together the inspiring stories of remarkable businesswomen from around the world. This book is a tapestry of diverse experiences woven together by the common thread of manifesting dreams and transforming lives.

BECOMING THE MANIFESTING DIVA

As you turn these pages, you'll be invited into the lives of women who have faced incredible challenges and triumphed. You'll read about near-death experiences that sparked a renewed zest for life, remarkable business growth achieved through sheer determination, and the overcoming of chronic health conditions that seemed insurmountable. Each story is a testament to the power of manifestation, showcasing how these women have consciously and unconsciously shaped their destinies.

One of the most beautiful aspects of this book is its practical approach. These women don't just share their stories; they also provide you with the tools and insights they used to manifest positive changes. From tips on setting clear intentions to techniques for maintaining a positive mindset, you'll find a wealth of knowledge that you can apply to your own life.

The authors of "Becoming the Manifesting Diva" have opened their hearts and shared their expertise, offering their support beyond the pages of this book. They are here to guide you, inspire you, and help you navigate your own journey of manifestation. Their stories are not just tales of personal triumph; they are blueprints for creating ripples of positive change in your life.

I believe that as you read these empowering narratives, you will find yourself resonating with the experiences of these women. Their stories will ignite your belief in the power of manifestation and inspire you to embrace the flow of the universe. You'll be encouraged to let go of what no longer serves you and to confidently pursue your dreams and ambitions.

FOREWORD BY DR. JOE VITALE

I personally know the publisher and lead author of this wonderful book. She's in my movie Zero Limits, and she's a beacon of light for men and women around the planet.

So, get comfortable, open your heart, and prepare to be inspired. "Becoming the Manifesting Diva" is not just a book; it's an invitation to transform your life, to create ripples of positive change, and to flow with the universe. Welcome to the journey of becoming your own manifesting diva.

Expect Miracles.

Dr. Joe Vitale

Table of Contents

FOREWORD i

Invitation to Your Miracle i

INTRODUCTION 7

AMMA VENTELÄ 9

I AM a Manifesting Diva - Unveiling the Secrets of My Transformation 9

About the Author 22

DANIELLE DEMOSS 24

My Journey of Self-Discovery to Becoming a Manifesting Diva 24

About the Author 40

DIANE BOVALINO 42

Magical Steps Along the Way to My Dream Life 42

About the Author 53

GISELLE LORENA HURTADO 55

Pathways To Destiny 55

About the Author 70

JO-ANNE ROSS 72

Return to Wholeness 72

About the Author 89

KARLA KOPP — 91

Creating Dreams Come True 91

About the Author 99

KATIE CAREY — 101

Manifesting Your Magical Life 101

About the Author 111

KATIE GAUTHIER — 113

Crossroads to Opportunities 113

About the Author 121

LOUISE SAMOSORN — 123

If You Believe, Then You Will Receive 123

About the Author 130

MARIE SCHLEMM — 131

Chocolate, Football, and the Tao 131

About the Author 144

REVEREND — 146

STACEY PIEDRAHITA — 146

The Little Reverend Who Could 146

About the Author 158

SUSANNE KURZ — 160

Becoming the Manifesting Diva with the Handbrake On 160

... 160

YANA WELLER 170

When You Ask, It Is Given ... 170

About the Author ... 178

ABOUT SOULFUL VALLEY PUBLISHING 180

INTRODUCTION

Welcome to *Becoming the Manifesting Diva: Creating Ripples While You Flow*, another remarkable book collaboration from Soulful Valley Publishing. We are thrilled to present this collection of captivating life stories shared by courageous businesswomen worldwide who have triumphed over adversity by consciously manifesting the life they desire.

Within the pages of this book, you will discover an array of diverse narratives illuminating the paths these authors have taken to manifest their dreams. They generously offer invaluable insights, tips, and tools that have empowered them to create the extraordinary lives they now lead – and to empower you to do the same.

With great pleasure, we welcome back international best-selling authors Dr Susanne Kurz, Karla Kopp, Amma Ventelä, Diane Bovalino, Giselle Lorena Hurtado, and, of course, yours truly's inclusion of another compelling chapter. Additionally, we are delighted to introduce new authors

BECOMING THE MANIFESTING DIVA

who are making their debut in this collaboration, adding fresh perspectives and experiences to the collection. We are all honoured and delighted that Dr. Joe Vitale has written a Foreword for us.

Becoming the Manifesting Diva delves into deeply vulnerable moments, allowing you to recognise that no matter how challenging your current circumstances may be, you have the power to transform your life by understanding the science behind the Laws of the Universe. While some concepts may seem counter-intuitive or defy logic, it is essential to remember that the universe operates with impeccable logic, aligning your reality with the energy, frequency, and vibration you emit. Your emotions play a pivotal role in this process, and this book encourages you to embrace the flow of positive and negative emotions rather than suppressing them. Doing so can redirect your life towards a new and fulfilling direction.

We eagerly await your feedback and encourage you to share your thoughts by leaving an Amazon review once you have immersed yourself in the wisdom within these pages. We intend to facilitate healing for as many women as possible, guiding them to reclaim the lives they were destined to live.

May this co-creation resonate deeply with your soul, regardless of your present circumstances. Embrace the journey and find solace in the transformative power of conscious manifestation.

Katie Carey
Soulful Valley Publishing

AMMA VENTELÄ

I AM a Manifesting Diva - Unveiling the Secrets of My Transformation

Manifesting My Soul Mission

I'm Amma, and I'm a Manifesting Diva! Have I always been? Yes, kind of. Have I learned to focus and manifest what I want? Yes! Let me share with you the things that I have learned.

I have lived most of my life – almost 50 years – without any knowledge or understanding of manifestation. I was never told about the law of attraction and was never made aware of my ability to create experiences and circumstances in my reality. I did everything I

BECOMING THE MANIFESTING DIVA

thought I was supposed to do and faithfully fulfilled the expectations of my culture, society, and family.

I was expected to go to school, graduate from higher education (university), get married, buy a house with a mortgage, have happy children, and achieve success in my profession. I was like an actress in my own life and focused on keeping everyone around me as happy as possible. I never even thought about stopping to consider my own dreams and goals. I just survived. Looking back on my life, I can see that on a material level, my life must have looked amazing and beautiful. Yet, all the time, I was aware of the misalignment, disharmony, and all-inclusive lack. I see now that I had fully forgotten who I was, as I was not consciously connected with my soul energy. I felt the separation and knew that I had missed something essential.

When I finally started to wake up spiritually in the 2010s, I quickly became clairvoyant. I found a connection to my spirit guides. I started to study spiritual wisdom and, of course, soon learned about the law of attraction and manifestation. My first tryouts were all about material needs: money, a new car, and even new clothes. I made a vision board with images of cars, travel destinations, etc. They were not successful.

However, another level of manifestation was going on. In August 2019, I was guided to participate in the Goal Mapping workshop (method of Brian Mayne), where my higher self and spirit guides were leading the process. I created the goal map with one clear goal: *International Lightworker*, the wise woo-woo woman. My person was totally surprised because I had no preliminary idea that I would like to become that. I thought I was in my dream profession, an aquatic ecologist saving the world's lakes and rivers. I was an international scientist with ambitious professional goals – not a woo-woo woman. I was a supervisor of several employees and a leader of several international projects. I knew there was no way to combine these with the woo-woo woman who had just appeared in my reality. Yet, the goal map was there, and I had even set a date: *August 2020*.

In December 2019, I also participated in the Soul Dream Map workshop where my higher self and spirit guides - guided me through the process of creating this visual dream map, a powerful manifestation tool that includes my soul-level dreams. This method has been given to Finnish Lightworker Kristiina Haltia, who now connects people with their soul-level dreams.

But then, 2020 changed everything. The pandemic changed everything in our world and my life. My work community broke down. We were all stuck working at home, and all social events – including the trips – were canceled. I was guided to participate in several spiritual courses, and they filled my spare time. Finally, in March 2020, I saw something that took my breath away: an International Lightworker course! The mentor there was Anu Grace, a woman I knew already. I immediately signed up and knew that something really important was starting.

The course lasted for four months, and during that time, I learned my first healing modality. I practiced with my international fellow students and learned to trust my ability to work in English

BECOMING THE MANIFESTING DIVA

(Finnish is my first language). I learned that in this way of connecting online with customers, I was fully guided by the Divine and able to channel the Source energies needed. I also learned how to start a business, market, and connect with customers. I had my first paying international customer in August 2020 – the exact date of my goal plan!

My manifestation also found new ways in 2020. I started having a manifestation diary where I wrote about my manifestation dreams daily. I became aware of the lack in my life: the lack of joy, the lack of light, and the lack of abundance. So, my manifestation took the form I AM JOY, I AM LIGHT, I AM ABUNDANCE. When the Lightworker course progressed, I added I AM LIGHTWORKER. There was even a beautiful Declaration of Lightwork in the course material, and I listened to it daily. I had no idea how the transformation from scientist to lightworker could happen in real life. I just recognized the deepest and strongest soul-level manifestation there could be.

I have told my transformation story in the book *Evolving on Purpose: Co-creating with the Divine* (Soulful Valley, 2023), so I will only tell the quick version here. The Universe showed me the way to step away from my science career. I resigned from my 21-year position in December 2021, and since then, I have been a full-time Lightworker.

Ok, you may now think that this was the end of the story—happily ever after. Well, not quite.

AMMA VENTELÄ

Me, Becoming the Manifesting Diva

I know nothing about manifestation!

I started my Lightworker journey with high hopes and Divine guidance. However, my person – my ego – was still in charge, especially in all money-related issues (which were many). I had been in an employee position all my life. Someone had paid some money to my bank account every single month, even during the holidays and sick leaves—our household with five members used to have that money. Now, I was on my own, and it was not easy to make income every single month.

There have been easy moments and extremely difficult moments. In the fall of 2022, I was in the middle of one of those challenging periods. I met Katie Carey in some of Joanna Hunter's courses. Katie mentioned that there would be a book called *Becoming a Manifesting Diva*. All of me shouted, "YES! I want to become a Manifesting Diva! Show me the way!" I finally had the financial resources to join the book project in January 2023.

This commitment guided me on the roller coaster ride of my life. Many times, I have felt like an ocean surfer in the tsunami waves. The bankruptcy of both my company and my personal economy has been nearly but Divinely prevented every time. I have had to learn to face my fears, trust my abilities, and value my worth.

In contrast to the challenges I faced during the first years of my lightworker career, 2023 was the most amazing, successful, and educational year ever. I created:

- Over 200k in sales for my company

BECOMING THE MANIFESTING DIVA

- Certificates from LightBringer, LightWebPriestess, and Akashic Record Reader trainings in Joanna Hunter's the100 Program
- A two-week trip to Bali with Jonette Crowley to work with Dragon Ley lines
- A trip to Scotland with my hubby (his lifetime dream)
- I went on a trip to Mallorca with my daughter and worked there with Mediterranean Sean and Ley lines.
- Wonderful courses, meditations, and VIP-coaching sessions for my customers
- Four amazing retreats
- Resources and implementation plans for the Egypt trip in February 2024 and Peru in August 2024
- Happiness in family life

Me, the Manifesting Diva

Since the spring of 2023, I have been guided to understand and embody the energy of surrender. Although I had learnt a lot about manifestation, I was still trying to manage and figure things out with the power of my ego and mind. I was trying to tell the Universe that I need this and this amount of money by this date. I also tried to figure out how to solve the situation all the time. I was working hard, and always – even in the most difficult and challenging situations – I was able to make the money I needed - in the exact moment that I needed it. But in those situations, I was far from the energy of ease and joy, which was my aim.

Also, in certain situations, I was limiting myself by saying, "Oh, I can't afford that!" or "That is not for me," meaning that I didn't believe I was worthy of those experiences. In March 2023, one of my students told me about the trip to Bali with the "Indiana Jones of the spiritual world," Jonette Crowley. She was organizing the trip to work with the Dragon Ley lines. I received the trip info, saw the price, and immediately excluded the whole idea. "No, that's way too expensive. It's not for me!" I had already forgotten about the trip, but then, one night, I was woken up by my spirit guides.

"Amma, check out that Bali trip again!"

"No! It's too expensive!" I answered.

"You have to read it again, and you have to go to Bali," they said.

"So how would that be possible?" I asked.

They explained that I should make a Facebook live the next day, talk about this possibility, the trip, and the ley lines, and ask if anyone would be willing to join me virtually. This was not the first time my guides asked me to speak publicly, but the topic this time was very strange, so you can imagine that my person was yelling, "Noooo! You can't do this! Nobody does anything like this!" But I did it.

As soon as I woke up, I made a post saying that I was going to go live later that day and asked, "Please join me!" I started the Facebook live as agreed, first hesitating and a person on alert, but then the words started to flow naturally. I felt the increasing excitement of the audience, and when I came to the point of asking them to participate, several people immediately answered, "Of course!" "I'm in!" and "Yes, you have to go! I'll support you." In half an hour, it was clear that there would be enough supporters to make the trip happen!

The Bali trip was full of pure bliss, moment after moment. I learned that I struggle to receive all the good in my life. I felt that I was not worthy of all those gifts, although it was clear that I was in the right place with the right people. I met my soul sister, Lorna, in Bali, and she told me again and again to focus on receiving. We did an amazing rafting tour in the crystal clear river, surrounded by the jungle and waterfalls. The beauty of the moment was unbelievable. "Amma, stop! Look! We have created this moment! Now, just receive." Lorna whispered. She also gave me the affirmation "Money flows effortlessly to me," which I have been using and learning since that moment.

I also learned that I easily think, "Well, thank you. This was great, and I understand this was more than enough for me. I am content with this, and I understand that it is rude to ask for more." However, when I reject the gifts of the Universe, I'm denying myself the opportunity for infinite abundance.

After Bali and other happy events, I often found myself with these limiting beliefs until I was guided to find the power of surrender. I started to focus on gratitude every day: "Thank you for all the gifts that I have received. I am content, and I'm ready to open myself even more. Show me how all this could be even more amazing and wonderful. I'm open and available for the highest manifestation of my soul purpose!"

This affirmation was a game-changer! I started to create each month with gratitude, joy, and excitement. I named the months in advance, like SuperSeptember, November of Light, December of Love and Peace, etc. I created events that I really wanted to organize and implemented them in total Divine guidance, surrendering and receiving – and they all were successful!

Show me how amazing this can be!

Since last summer, I have consistently lived this philosophy: "Thank you and show me – just for fun – how much more amazing this can be!" My life has been full of miracles. There is no time or space to share them all here, but there is one specific miracle that I want to share with you.

One of my 2023 manifestation topics was a trip to Egypt. I knew that the Finnish Lightworker colleagues would organize a trip there. Originally, the trip was supposed to take place in November 2023, but it was moved to February 2024. I knew I was supposed to be there for something really important. The topic I was given before the trip was the throat chakra of the Earth in Luxor. I have been working with ley lines and Earth chakras before and knew there would be challenging energies to clear. Just before the trip, I also received the downloads of Energies of Peace and Oneness, which we were supposed to anchor to Egypt. Again, I had a virtual group to support me both economically and energetically. There were 21 people on the physical trip and 43 virtually.

We received a beautiful set of light codes and activations in the Giza pyramids and sphinx. I was surprised when I was guided to channel a long and quite detailed message to our group. I had channeled only a couple of times earlier for my own use.

Then something totally unexpected happened. On the morning of our second day of travel, I chose to have breakfast with one of my fellow travelers, a man I didn't know. We introduced ourselves, shared the work we do, and found surprising similarities. We agreed that it might be fun to do a session exchange sometimes. I thought it might be sometime after the trip. However, my guides prompted me to sit next to him during the long bus drive, and I was asked if we had some shared past lives. I got the information that this was our ninth shared human life and the ninth shared soul experience. We became very curious about what that would mean.

Again, I opened my channel and asked. We were told that we are a working team with a soul contract to help Earth and humanity in ascension. We had agreed to incarnate to the same time and space at intervals to heal each other from the wounds of other lifetimes lived separately. This energetic structure aimed to prepare us for the ultimate service, which was this trip. We aimed to open and activate the ancient, broken energy portal of Oneness.

We received clear guidance for the task. First, we healed each other for a couple of days just by sharing our life experiences and being close to each other during the bus trips. Then, we were informed that the portal of Oneness was in King's Valley, Luxor. There, we did powerful energy clearings and were guided to step into a certain place at a very specific moment. We learnt that the moment we were in our full power together was a cosmic code that activated a vast operation around the portal activation.

The moment was unbelievable, and we really felt the strong energy shift. The activation meant that the time of cosmic separation was over, and there was now an open portal for cosmic communication and cooperation again.

We learnt that activating the Portal of Oneness made it possible to do other important activations. We opened the connection of very ancient feminine Polaria energy (originating from Ursa Major and Stella Polaris constellations) and the Dendera temple of Hathor. We also cleared and opened the throat chakra of Earth in Luxor, as I knew before the trip. However, the most powerful task was to create and activate a new portal of peace to the Red Sea and anchor it to Sharm el Sheik. Of course, we didn't do this alone, but together with the whole group of travelers, both virtual and physical. This work has just begun, and I can't wait to see how it unfolds in the future. Our mission was given and guided by the Cosmic Council of Oneness, who I will be channeling more soon.

For me, the greatest gift of the trip was Heikki Lackström, artist, master healer, and my cosmic work partner in the most challenging service works for Mother Earth. I was happy with my soul mission before this, but I kept asking, "Please show me how this could be even more amazing," and I received him! He has already

BECOMING THE MANIFESTING DIVA

healed me physically and mentally, and I can't wait to work and experience adventures with him again in the future. We are working globally with the major ley lines and energy portals. We already started in Peru in August – but that's another story!

Thank you, Universe! All this is already perfect, but I'm open and available to experience it all, so please show me how this can be even more amazing.

Summary

Successful manifestation is <u>NOT</u> about:
- asking for stuff (like a new car) and the Universe giving it to me
- desperately needing things (like money to pay bills)
- setting strict deadlines for the Universe
- solving the problems myself and giving instructions to the Universe
- holding on to my negative stories and beliefs
- my ego leading the process

Successful manifestation is, more than anything, a vibrational match! You attract what you are. When I surround myself with the energy of gratitude and align myself to my highest Self, Source, and Earth, I AM JOY, I AM LIGHT, and I AM ABUNDANCE. I am. And I open myself to all of this. I give myself permission to receive all the gifts there are for me. I trust that all I need will come to me with ease and grace. I can trust that every moment is the highest manifestation of my soul's purpose.

And so it is.

About the Author

*A**mma Ventelä*** is a channel of Divine cosmic energies, an intuitive psychic, and a spiritual healer living in Finland. She is the CEO of her fast-growing spiritual business, Thyra&Me Oy, named after Viking Queen Thyra, one of her spirit guides and her real-life great-grandmother from 32 generations ago.

She has a PhD in ecology, and for 25 years, she was fully devoted to an international aquatic science career. In the 2010s, she experienced a transformational spiritual awakening that turned her from a work-oriented, stressed-out, joyless woman to a happy, inspired, and enthusiastic queen of woo-woo energy.

Amma has received full downloads of spiritual courses and programs since 2021. The Academy of Joy and Light has already more than 200 students and both her personal mentoring and the group sessions with clairvoyant energy healing are currently very popular.

She is now remembering the Lemurian way of connecting with ley lines and healing them by singing and chanting. She has a weekly service meditation for this on Facebook, and people are joining the public live event from different parts of the world. She is offering both group and 1:1 sessions for healing and coaching.

Connect with Amma below:

- https://www.ammaventela.com

DANIELLE DEMOSS

My Journey of Self-Discovery to Becoming a Manifesting Diva

I grew up and lived most of my life in Renton, a beautiful valley city south of the "Emerald City" in the shadow of Mount Rainer, minutes from Lake Washington and the Cedar River, and roughly two hours from fresh mountain air or the Pacific Ocean. I was always drawn to nature, especially water, but could always get my occasional city vibe fix, dashing around the bustling city of Seattle thirty minutes away. Since I was a child, I've always been intuitive and had an innate desire to help others and to share my insights with others. When I was young, my dad was a vice president at a local college and was also on the negotiating team that negotiated teacher contracts for the school district; my mom stayed home to care for me and my older brother. My parents never talked about financial things in front of me and my brother, but I could tell when times were good or tough.

When times were good financially, we'd have lots of different foods, and I'd be able to participate in a lot of activities. My mom was a great cook who loved to make different foods, especially Italian recipes from my dad's family or something new she'd seen in a magazine. I'd get to participate in soccer, softball, gymnastics, swimming and Girl Scouts; I'd go swimming at the local pools or rivers and to the movies with my friends. We'd go out to dinner once a week and even go on vacations as a family.

When we didn't have as much money, we'd eat macaroni and cheese with hot dogs, tomato soup and grilled cheese, canned chili with hot dogs, fried rice (rice and whatever-is-left-over-in-the-fridge), some Shepherd's pie (a little bit of hamburger, canned green beans, canned corn, and mashed potatoes) or breakfast for dinner (eggs and toast or pancakes). Those were the times I remember my parents would say things regarding money, such as, "That's too expensive! We can't afford that!" or "Stop wasting that! Money doesn't grow on trees! Your dad works hard for our money."

I had no real concept of money (or manifestation), so I decided as a kid that I would grow up, make lots of my own money, and spend it on whatever I wanted. I started babysitting when I was 12, and then at 15, I began lifeguarding. I would spend my money as fast as I made it, and my dad would shake his head and say, "I swear!

BECOMING THE MANIFESTING DIVA

Money burns a hole in your pocket. You spend it all, and you never save any. What happens when you want to go do something after you've spent all your money, or you want a car someday? When you don't have two pennies to rub together, don't come to ask us for money every time you don't have enough. You need to learn to save your money for a rainy day." Unbeknownst to them, or to me for that matter, my parents instilled the first stories of lack.

I went to college for two years, then took that proverbial "one-year break" that turned into what seemed like a permanent hiatus. I wanted to live independently and not be told when to come home or what to do with my money. I was an adult, and I wanted to be able to do what I wanted. Boy, was I in for a rude awakening!

I got a full-time job and moved into my first apartment with a roommate, no washer, no dryer, and no dishwasher. I triumphantly thought I had it made; I could do whatever I wanted now – until the utility bills started to come in, and the rent was due, or I needed groceries or gas – and oh yeah, my car insurance was due.

"Ugh, I don't have the money to wash my clothes this week, so I'll have to go to Mom and Dad's… hmmm… Maybe I will eat there too because it's way better than what I have at home." Money went out as fast as it came in, but it certainly wasn't on the things I envisioned spending it on. I was struggling to pay all my bills, but there was certainly never enough for anything else. Unless I chose to skip a bill to splurge on something or go out with friends for one night, I would justify it by telling myself that I deserved it because, after all, I'd worked hard for my money.

Then, not paying that bill would somehow snowball, making things even harder on myself later.

This is not how I pictured being an adult. *Is that all there is to adult life? Working hard and paying bills?* I thought to myself. *There has to be more to life than this.*

Then, I discovered credit cards. I finally found my answer! *I could use credit cards for gas or some of my bills until my next check, for that TV that I really wanted, or to go out with my friends. Oh, and maybe a road trip! I'll pay it with my next check—or my check after that. All I have to do is pay the minimum, right? I'll pay the rest later.*

I figured out that if I consistently paid the minimum on the first card, then other creditors would give me cards too – with higher limits. I thought I'd discovered the answer to all my problems. Now, I had plastic if I wanted to buy something or do something if I didn't have enough from my paycheck (which seemed to be most – if not all – of the time.) And I only had to pay the minimum on each card. I could pay the rest later, no biggie.

Not long after that, I got my first car loan on a brand-new car. Yes! I falsely believed buying a new car meant no more unexpected repairs.

Now, I will just have to worry about making a regular car payment which I thought has to be less than all the repairs that my old car needed. Besides, this new car looks a lot nicer than my ugly beater car that always broke down.

Of course, I hadn't given the slightest thought to the "save for a rainy day" concept my dad had mentioned. Everything was great. I bought a few things for the apartment when I saw things I liked, some new cute clothes here and there, and I always had money for gas. Oh, and I could go to a movie or dinner and drinks with my friends whenever I wanted. This is how the financial game worked!

Little did I know that my hard-learned lesson in compound interest and the truth about credit cards had just begun. The subtle lesson was picking up speed rapidly as the balances grew. I had to start juggling the bills, and within a few months, the balls began to drop. My no-longer-subtle-lesson was about to show up fiercely, front and center in my face, not to be ignored.

Unable to keep up with the payments and late fees on maxed-out accounts, I started losing cards as lenders closed my accounts and, with them, my self-esteem. I had to curb my lifestyle dramatically. As my dad said, I had a "champagne taste on a beer budget." Champagne was no longer on the menu. Words from my childhood like "That's too expensive" or "I can't afford that" became part of my regular vocabulary. "Money certainly doesn't grow on trees."

I'd get a raise in my department store loss prevention job, and the small increase would help, but never seemed to be enough to really matter.

I work hard for my money, but no matter what I do, it's never enough.

I perceived life as a struggle and told myself, "That's just the way life is, and it's never going to be easy." The idea of "never enough" became a common theme in my life.

Romantic relationships weren't working out for me, either. I was a consummate people pleaser who struggled with healthy boundaries and made excuses for red flags in men. When the relationship would inevitably end, I always felt I was treated wrongly or unfairly instead of seeing these failed relationships as an opportunity to become more self-aware. I thought that failing in love and life meant that I was a complete failure, instead of viewing my failures as opportunities to teach me something new about myself so that I could change my narrative.

I spiraled into more and more negative self-talk, which brought me further into lack and into the "my life sucks" mentality. With my self-esteem tanked, I perceived myself as not good enough to make better money, not good enough to be in a better relationship or with a man who didn't cheat on me or have nice things.

As the negative thoughts and beliefs perpetuated my "that's just the way it is" mindset, I settled for less than I deserved. I allowed this dangerous and toxic mindset to defeat me and destroy my dreams. Negativity became my new normal, and I became hopeless and helpless. I stopped allowing myself to dream, even little dreams, or to think that my life could be different.

It would take almost two decades, two failed marriages, many years as a single mom of a special needs child, two long-distance moves, and filing for bankruptcy before I started to become self-aware. I became aware of the fact that decades of my life had passed, and I didn't have anything to show for them. My core family – my parents, my brother, and even my bio dad and stepmom were successful from my point of view in that they had houses, cars, financial stability, and went on vacations, etc. What was I doing wrong?

I worked hard, tried to be responsible, and paid my bills, but there still never seemed to be enough. I spent many years in service and managerial positions but always felt something was missing. I tried to be a good person and a good friend, but I put other people before myself most of the time or just went along with whatever everyone else wanted.

Even though my son never went without (thanks to the generosity of his grandparents), I still wanted to show him that there was more to life than the way we were living it. I wanted to have more instead of just settling for less, but I didn't know how to change anything. I was tired of being tired. I was tired of feeling behind the eight ball. I wanted to do more fun things, not just necessary things. I became aware of how I felt every day, physically and emotionally. I wanted to put on a happy face every day and be thankful for what I had, but I wasn't truly happy. I had mastered the "fake it til you make" type of happy façade. I wanted to feel energized, but instead, I felt exhausted and depressed. I felt that I was not good enough in many areas of my life and couldn't figure out how to be "enough."

I felt obligated to be there for my son, family, friends, and everyone else because that's what a good person does: putting others' needs before their own. Sometimes, I'd say "yes" when everything in me was telling me to say "no."

There were times I'd feel resentful and occasionally even mad. Then, I'd feel guilty and beat myself up for feeling like I didn't have enough empathy and compassion for others, and I didn't want others to think I was selfish. But I was feeling drained, like I'd lost my voice – or worse yet, I had lost myself. No one really cared anyway.

I started to become more and more aware of things I thought or said to myself. Most of it wasn't very positive or nice. I would never speak to my friends or family that way, and I would never allow someone else to speak to me that way, so why was I willing to accept that from myself? I did not seem to have an ounce of understanding or compassion for myself, but I had an abundant supply of compassion for others.

Did the negative self-talk and mindsets about myself and my life create my unhappiness? Did my negative perceptions unknowingly set me up for negative expectations? Did the negative thoughts and expectations influence my beliefs and behaviors, essentially causing them to come to fruition? I dwelled on the negative in my mind, so I had gotten negative back in my life. Maybe it was time to really evaluate where these negative thoughts came from and what my beliefs truly are.

I began an intense process of serious self-reflection for the first time in my life. I realized that my beliefs, thoughts, and self-talk produced my emotions, and my actions and reactions resulted from my emotional state. I had unconsciously created identities that perpetuated limiting beliefs, negative thoughts, and self-talk. Every time I was triggered by something, my negative thoughts produced disempowering emotions, which in turn dictated my subsequent actions (or inactions), thus creating my reality. I discovered that what you choose to focus your thoughts on expands, and you end up receiving more of it. My thoughts had become my outcome. The light bulb had come on!

I had been living unconsciously, perpetuating false identities that I had created in my mind and total misalignment with my true self. This realization started my journey into self-discovery to find my personal truth, fully uncover my passion and purpose, create a different life, and manifest my dreams.

But who was I now? I knew I had some core values, but what did I truly desire? I had stopped dreaming so long ago because I had been so defeated, figuring my dreams were so unattainable back then that they could never possibly be my reality. I started reading books and taking self-development classes. I started to allow myself to dream just a little. I knew I had to start with self-love. I had been so harsh and critical of myself in the past; I was trying to help others while running on empty, which caused me to become easily irritated or react from an emotional place.

In the last two decades, I lost my confidence and true identity; I wasn't standing up for myself or speaking my truth. I had to find my voice and be more loving to myself. Only then could I start speaking my truth and learning to have compassion for myself. In practicing self-love, I learned to set healthy boundaries with others; I gained self-confidence and learned to respect, have compassion, and trust myself. I became aware that I started to genuinely feel happier.

I started to think "what if" and started journaling small dreams and goals.

In my journey of self-discovery, to live in alignment with myself, I also had to look at my values, virtues, and identities – loyalty, honesty, responsibility, respect, integrity, kindness, and compassion. I was loyal, kind, respectful, patient, and honest with others, but I had to learn to be those things to myself. There were other values I wanted to develop – positivity and optimism with myself, not just with others. I wanted to master diligence and perseverance if I was going to define my dreams and go after them.

Next, I began to unravel the identities I had created with the different stories I told myself, limiting beliefs, patterns, and habits. I had created a lot of them. Where did they come from? Were they even mine? I had created stories that I had been "hard done by", stories that I had perpetually gotten the "short end of the stick", or stories that it was "poor little me," stories that money wasn't easy to come by or that you had to work hard for money. Stories about how life was hard and that you didn't get anything in this world without hard work.

Then there was the one that I wasn't good enough, and everyone else had more than me. Last but not least, my deeply entrenched people-pleaser always told the story that I had to do it myself because no one else was going to do it. I was missing self-love and self-worth; I didn't trust myself and certainly didn't accept myself.

BECOMING THE MANIFESTING DIVA

All these things manifested the lack of abundance in all areas of my life – lack of money, love, lack of enough on any level. All these lack mindsets blocked my ability to receive. How was I going to release these blocks? Once I determined the identities/stories I had been telling myself, I had to look deeper at the limiting beliefs, traumas, and negative patterns. I had to learn to identify my negative triggers that produced the thoughts that brought up the limiting beliefs, which in turn brought on the disempowering emotions.

I learned that our emotions are our body's compass that tells us if we're in alignment or out of alignment. If the feeling is not good, you're out of alignment, which puts you in what is called lack energy. There are two types. Once I was aware of my negative emotions, I could learn to stop and interrupt the pattern before I made any decisions and subsequent actions that would put me further in lack. I asked myself, "What can I control?" and I focused solely on that. Because what I focus on expands, I had to get back to at least a neutral emotion so that I could make better choices.

I learned that what I think, feel, and do takes me to a higher or a lower vibration. That creates my experience and thus determines my reality. Lower emotions calibrate to lower vibrations and bring about manifestations in some form of lack. Higher emotions calibrate to higher vibrations that bring about manifestations more in line with abundance.

So, I built supporting self-love and self-care routines while trying to become more aware of my negative triggers and stop myself somewhere in my pattern to see it from a higher perspective with love and light (which is not always easy). I try to bring my feelings and emotions to a neutral level to stop my vibration from going lower, and I try to make decisions and take actions that are in alignment with my true self and for the highest good.

I started journaling and shining a light on any false identities, expanding my beliefs (exposing myself to the opposite of my limiting belief), having better self-talk, and learning to dream bigger. I am learning to recognize negative triggers and stop the pattern somewhere in my thoughts and emotions to try to get to a neutral or more empowering emotion and, thus, a higher vibrational state. I learned to include daily practices to raise my vibrations – gratitude journaling, meditation, positive thinking, breathwork, visualization, affirmations, acts of kindness, and service to others. I get out to connect with nature whenever I can. Happiness and abundance didn't seem so elusive anymore.

Now that I was setting goals and journaling big dreams, I wanted to learn how to manifest them. I'd heard of the Law of Attraction, but I couldn't figure out why it didn't seem to work for me. Then I heard a mentor say that actions were still required. So, I would say prayers and set intentions. Then I noticed there were signs, such as numbers, that would show up (222, 333, 444, 1010, 1212, etc.) or other synchronicities or feelings. There could be other things too – songs, animals, technology issues, etc. These are not coincidences; they are signs. These are what I needed to act on.

I try to pay attention to signs because they can show the next step, which might be better than what I thought the next step would be. I learned to surrender my will and acquiesce to God/the Universe that they will send whatever is in the highest good. So, I continued to say my prayers, set my intentions, work through my triggers, and try to keep my emotions positive, concentrating on love so I can stay in a higher vibrational state, making me a vibrational match for what I am trying to manifest.

While I will perpetually be a work in progress, like peeling back layers of an onion, with self-development, personal growth, and manifestation, I am proud to share that in an eight-month period of 2020; I manifested the perfect apartment in the exact school district that I wanted along with my perfect car and the second income stream to afford the apartment and the car payment. My intentions were literally to manifest the perfect car and perfect apartment for me and the additional income stream to afford everything so that my family had enough.

I had faith that my intentions would manifest and surrendered that God/Universe would send me what was perfect for me. I didn't know what that was going to look like. The car that I manifested was three years old, had low mileage, and was exactly the car I desired to own in my favorite car color - wine/burgundy - and included the top-of-the-line package. I probably shouldn't have qualified for it based on my credit score, but the financing went through, and I received the exact payment I could afford.

As my state started to come off the rent moratorium imposed during covid, not many rentals were available. I needed a three-bedroom apartment in a specific school district so my son could stay at his school, but rent had gone so high that I also needed a supplemental income stream to afford it. The second income stream came through just before an apartment complex two miles from my son's school called to let me know a three-bedroom unit was available within my price range – and even included a garage! I didn't even need to rent a storage unit anymore. It was the perfect place.

In 2022, I had been at my program administrator job for five and a half years. I loved the department and team I worked with and got to work from home, but I needed to make more money with the rising costs in this post-Covid economy. Advancements in my department were limited because hardly anyone ever left. Our department was a very sought-after department in which to work. The best options for a potential salary increase at my current company were applying for sales positions or the infrequently open management positions outside my department at one of my company's local branch offices. Neither were jobs I was really interested in. It would be a huge stretch for one of the two program manager positions in my department to open up, as the people in those positions had been there many years, and no one mentioned any desire to leave. So, for me to obtain a program manager-type position, I would need to look outside of the company. I didn't really want to go outside my company where I would most likely have to return to an office and lose three weeks of vacation. Still, I set the intention to manifest the perfect job for me and surrendered, having faith that God/Universe would send me what was best for me. I started applying for positions but was very picky about which ones I applied for. I only applied for positions that gave me the feeling of a full body "yes!"

All of a sudden, my supervisor, who had been with the company for 25 years, got an offer from another company that he couldn't refuse. One of the program managers was promoted to his position. The vacant program manager position was in the southern part of the state, so it wasn't feasible for me as I was in the northern part of the state, and I needed to stay where I was for my son to finish school.

Besides, my new supervisor knew me but didn't really know my skills or everything that I did for our department yet, so he would not have considered me for a program manager position at that time. He filled the southern program manager spot. I continued to apply to other places, having faith that the perfect position would manifest.

Eight months later, a management position presented itself. It was a lot more money than I was making, but it was forty-five minutes away from working in the office for another company. I decided to take it even though I was sad to leave my current team.

I called my supervisor to let him know that I had received a job offer from another company and would send him an email putting in my two weeks' notice. There was a long period of silence, and my supervisor responded that I was the third person out of the four people on our management team to give notice in less than 24 hours.

My supervisor had discovered that I was not just an administrator and that I not only knew much more about the processes and flows of this department than the other program managers (or even he did) but that I had created some of the internal processes. It became evident that this department flowed and functioned well because of me, so he did not want to see me leave, which would have created great hardship for him. So, I applied for the north program manager position in my own department and, with the salary and the bonus package, I manifested a $29,000 a year raise working fewer hours than I did as a program administrator, and I kept my three weeks of vacation.

In my continued self-development and "peeling of my onion layers," I feel called to service others. I have launched a spiritual life coaching and healing business to help others clear their blocks and manifest their dreams.

About the Author

Danielle DeMoss is an energy healer certified in multiple modalities and an Akashic Records Intuitive Guide and Reader. She is a certified Practitioner in Geo Love Healing, a Lightbringer Coach and Healer, and a LightWeb Priestess Coach and Healer; both the latter are based on LightWeb®, which is a Soul-Based Ascension Technology.

Danielle believes that every person is here for a divine purpose and is on a journey to bring their light to the world by learning to embody their truth and empower themselves to live what lights them up. Since she was a child, she has always been intuitive and had an innate desire to help others and to always share with or teach others all she has learned.

She has a dual Bachelor's in Criminal Justice and Human Services, and her purpose and passion are to help others on their life journey through various energy-healing modalities and to help them discover ways in which they are hindering their ability to shine their light to the fullest, how to empower themselves, and how to manifest their dreams.

DANIELLE DEMOSS

Danielle is inspired daily by her son who is learning to live his best life with the challenges of Autism and ADHD. In her spare time, she enjoys going to movies with her son, reading, traveling, trying new foods, and taking classes in other metaphysical-based service modalities. She is developing and launching her spiritually-based business online, so she may be of service to more people.

Connect with Danielle below:
- Email: danielle@danielledemoss.com
- Website: https://danielledemoss.com

DIANE BOVALINO

Magical Steps Along the Way to My Dream Life

We are all born with magic in us. It is sprinkled into our chakra system – the energy channels in our body – while we are in our mother's womb. The key to creating the magical life that will meet your wildest dreams is to unlock your magic as you grow into becoming an adult. Before we can understand that we are deserving of this magnificent life, we need to release any and all limiting beliefs that have conditioned us to accept a "normal" life.

I started manifesting my dream life after my fight with breast cancer because I could no longer live a "normal life." Now, I have the desire, passion, and drive to obtain "That Dream Life". A year and a half after the immediate treatments from breast cancer ended, the magic in my chakra system was flowing freely throughout the major seven energy wheels coming alive, especially in the Root, Sacral, and Solar Plexus. With that said, my three lower chakras – also known as the "lower triangle" – held most of my magic at that time. They govern our physical and emotional identity with our relationship to the physical world.

The first deep intention for my dream life was to find a driving force back in my career because working in a leadership position in Information Technology (IT) was no longer fulfilling. I would find time to sit quietly in the evening under the new moon and full moon each month, connecting into my three lower chakras and tuning into my soul purpose in life to find my authentic self. During the new moon, which is the time to manifest, I would receive downloads of data and images on areas to focus on for my dream job, career, business, and a new line of work for ultimate happiness, success, and joy.

The full moon period allowed a sacred time to release blocks, express gratitude, and share specific key items to let go of before I could move into my life's passion and purpose, the place where I was meant to shine my light on the World and be in my sovereignty.

The main theme threaded throughout the data and images coming in the new moon phase was highlighting a new profession in helping others. I would see image downloads of a nurse, counselor, yoga instructor, and energy healer. I also meditated during the deep dive period, searching into my soul to locate my new passion and purpose in my solar plexus.

BECOMING THE MANIFESTING DIVA

When I began my yoga practice in my 30s, I dreamed of getting certified to teach yoga. I had no idea how that was ever going to come to fruition. During meditations, I would see myself writing a book and sharing my story in order to help others. After going through breast cancer, I was driven to use my experience to help other women rise above and win their own battles against cancer.

When the full moon was out, I would sit patiently in meditation with my bare feet in the grass to pick up the blocks that needed to be released, found in the root, sacral, heart, and crown chakras. When the root chakra is balanced, we feel grounded and secure in connecting to our physical identity. My root chakra needed to release blocks because the breast cancer treatment really wreaked havoc on this energy wheel.

The sacral chakra held feelings of lack of self-worth due to limited time for pleasure and creativity during cancer treatment. After the loss of my breasts from the double mastectomy, my heart chakra was holding severe blocks, which severed the connection to my core soul and caused an incongruence.

The seventh chakra, the crown, which allows us to connect to our life's purpose and spirituality, held areas in it with blocks from all of the treatment I went through during breast cancer. The good news is that during the full moon meditations, I received streams of consciousness telling me the specific items to release to clear all blocks and allow me to move into my magical life. The answer was clear to me. In order to light the fire in my soul that fueled my engine clearly, I needed to move into a world of helping others and leave my successful career in the IT world. I had no idea how this would come to shape in the physical form, so I decided to give the plan over to the Divine, and in the meantime, I would continue to manifest my dream life.

A yearly activity that is a foundational element of manifestation for me is creating my vision board. I keep it simple by gathering old magazines, purchasing a colorful poster board, and ensuring I have a strong craft glue to paste all of the images on the poster board. The next step is finding the images that I am manifesting into my dream life. *What are my goals, desires, and intentions for that year?* I ask myself before I begin to start tackling the pages in the pile of magazines. Then, I take action by cutting out images from the magazines that will meet the goals, desires, and intentions I outlined for the year: places I want to travel, a house by the ocean, *and* a picture of a purse overflowing with money. An abundance of financial freedom is key to obtaining many of the items on the vision board and, most importantly for me, positive words of intention.

Once my vision board is complete, it is very important to find a place to hang it in my home. I always find a place in my home each year where I will see it when I wake up and before I go to bed.

By seeing the visual representation of my goals daily, I will keep my brain focused on my goals and, in turn, rewire my brain for success. In the end, the images and words manifest my dream life through the vision board. The vision board centers around the *law of attraction*: the idea that the universe will provide you with whatever you focus on in your life. I focus on my daily images of a beach house, and a purse of money, along with positive statements. For instance, one statement says, "I am a winner," which is exactly what I will receive in my dream life.

Another step in my manifestation journey that is very symbolic and, at the same time, actual documentation of my manifestation story of creating my magical life is the creation of my two Troll bracelets. I have named each one of the bracelets Freedom and Ocean. My Freedom bracelet is defined as the freedom to live the life that meets my wildest dreams, free from limiting beliefs, failure, and fear. The Ocean bracelet is a reminder that I will own a house by the ocean one day as I believe in my hopes, dreams, and aspirations.

I purchase a Trollbead at specific points on my manifestation journey. It could be specifically to attract that item or to document an important goal met towards my dream life. I wear both Troll bracelets frequently as a reminder of my manifestation journey towards this blissful life I am creating daily. With each purchased Troll bead, I see it as a talisman also on my manifestation journey. The Troll bracelets are a tangible visual manifestation element for me that I have throughout the day to focus on and give me the clarity to wire my brain for success as a second step after the vision board.

In the spring of 2018, a friend asked me if I wanted to learn Reiki healing with her since I was continuing my journey to my dream life. I had received Reiki treatments after my immediate treatments for breast cancer when the surgery was over, and chemotherapy (the next major step) was upon me. I was trying to understand how to live this life with the daily fear of a recurrence, along with accepting my newly defined body that I had to choose in order to stay in the physical world.

Reiki healing was a catalyst that springboarded me into action in life and put the spark back in my eyes. After one weekend, I learned Reiki 1 and 2. I was hooked on this healing power as a Reiki healer. Three months later, I became a Reiki Master while allowing the Divine to lead the way to my dream life, and I continued to manifest with intention and goal setting.

I spent the next year and a half performing Reiki healing on myself, my family, and my friends, strengthening my skill set with Reiki healing. An additional skill I now hold in my manifestation treasure chest is Reiki. I use Reiki now to manifest since Reiki is a wonderful way to bring Divine guidance into your life and to guide your manifesting process. For specific goals that I want to manifest in my life, I write the specific goal on individual index cards and place Reiki on the cards between my hands daily in the morning and evening. I have added this practice to my morning and evening vision board review. I recall that one specific goal listed on one of my index cards was to open a business of my own one day, as this has been my dream since I was a young girl. I wrote this down in the summer of 2018 and continued to manifest it with Reiki energy daily on the card. In time, I reflected on the images that came through on the new moon downloads, and the Divine led me to open Lotus Soul Healing Arts, LLC, in November 2019. I manifested my business that day

BECOMING THE MANIFESTING DIVA

through Reiki, the Divine, vision boards, intention setting, new moon manifestation, and full moon releases.

I knew at that moment my manifestation journey had to continue because the Divine and my soul's purpose in life were just getting started. Every day, leading to new adventures in my healing business, I continued to use manifestation with Reiki to grow my client base as a new business owner. I focused on intention setting for the practice surrounding abundance for the Reiki practice in clients and finances. I saw a thriving practice on my horizon, always with the vision of helping clients at the center of the practice, the core. The practice's soul mission for manifestation threaded back to the new moon intentions of the images. I saw myself as an energy healer helping others. I followed the guidance I read in one of my Reiki manuals from the International Center of Reiki Training (ICRT), which I continue to perform today.

I say a prayer daily, which is: "Guide me and heal me so that I can be of greater service to others." By sincerely saying this prayer daily, I am opening my heart and path to receive help from the spiritual beings to guide me in my Reiki practice and my life purpose.

As time passed and I met more clients in my business, I was guided by spirit to teach Reiki. Many of my clients would ask me if I would teach Reiki, and all these questions were a sign from the universe that I must teach Reiki. Teaching Reiki filled my soul with passion as I increased the number of Reiki healers worldwide.

Now, Reiki is being spread across the universe thanks to my teaching, time, and passion. I had this burning desire to spread the word that if every family could have a Reiki practitioner, it would be a beautiful world. Every family would have an energy healer to call on during times of crisis to assist the collective family members as a whole.

I met my Yoga teacher through one of my Reiki clients. She told me that her daughter had a yoga studio, and she taught yoga at the 200-hour instructor level. She signed up for my upcoming Reiki 1 and 2 class and explained that her daughter wanted to join the class. She and I created a wonderful bond as she ended up certifying me as a 200-hour Yoga Instructor, and I certified her as a Holy Fire III online Reiki Master. The dream I had in my 30s to become a Yoga instructor came to fruition through manifestation, the Divine, and the direct use of universal life force energy: Reiki.

I saw myself writing a book with the downloads during the new moon manifestations. I thought the book would be about my journey through breast cancer to help other women in the fight. In July 2022, supporting my Yoga teacher, I visited the author site on a multi-author chapter book about Toxic Relationships. Spirit called me to apply because the publisher was still accepting additional authors. I was accepted, and now I am an international best-selling author with Soulful Valley Publishing in the book *Entangled No More*.

Spirit guided me to share about a toxic work relationship that I had broken free from, and now I am thriving like a phoenix from the ashes. Manifesting the desire to write a book is one thing, but I never dreamed of becoming an international best-selling author. It is amazing to see all the magnificent events in your life when you

BECOMING THE MANIFESTING DIVA

manifest your dream life. The universe brings you gifts that are surprises along your journey to always provide you with even more joy, excitement, and enthusiasm than we could imagine we would feel in this lifetime.

One new moon, I created my manifestation list as it was part of an assignment for a class I was taking, and even though I was traveling, this action needed to occur. I was in upstate New York at the time, visiting my parents. I decided to manifest a diamond ring that evening, and I wrote it on my list. Even though I had beautiful jewelry, I didn't have a diamond ring, and I had wanted one for a long time. I loved diamonds, and as a single woman, I knew I didn't need to wait to get engaged to have a ring on my hand. I had thought of buying one for myself for the last few years but never took action. Instead, I went outside with my list in hand under the new moon. I meditated and lit my list of intentions on fire under the new moon.

The next day, my mother gave me a pretty pink case. "Diane, I would like you to have this ring now. Will you wear it?"

I couldn't believe my eyes! I stared in shock at the diamond ring my father gave her for their engagement. I remembered my manifestation list from the night before and said, "Are you sure, Mom?"

She smiled. "Yes, I want you to have it. Try it on." She slipped her engagement ring onto my finger - a perfect fit! She called to my father, "Hon, come over here, and see the ring on Diane!" Now, I always wear my mother's ring on my right ring finger.

DIANE BOVALINO

My most recent manifestation creation in my life was winning a slot as a contributing author to the book *Becoming the Manifesting Diva*. I saw the book when Soulful Valley Publishing announced this creation, and they were looking for contributing authors. At the time, I held the intention to be one of the contributing authors out to the universe.

In the year 2023, Soulful Valley Publishing held a contest, and the winner would get to write a chapter as a contributing author in this book, *Becoming the Manifesting Diva*. I saw the opportunity, and I knew that was the universe providing me with the manifestation path, and I just needed to step on it. I started crossing off as many of the items I could submit for points in the contest. While I was waiting for the final announcement of the winner of the contest, I would frequently visualize my name being announced as the winner of the contest to receive a contributing author slot for *Becoming the Manifesting Diva* book, and I also felt the excitement energetically in my body as a winner.

I also visualized myself writing the chapter and began to think about what I was going to write.

The day came, and I received the news that I was the winner. I manifested this contributing chapter in *Becoming the Manifesting Diva*. I was so excited that my manifestation steps, intentions, and actions worked, and now I am able to share my "Magical Steps Along the Way to My Dream Life" in this book.

Traveling is my true passion and has resonated with my mind, body and soul from a very young age. I have always dreamed of

BECOMING THE MANIFESTING DIVA

traveling to Hawaii since I was a young girl. I have placed Hawaii on my vision board every year since I started with this manifestation process. In 2022, I purchased the *Law Of Attraction Planner*, which I have added in as another tool for manifesting. I placed Hawaii as Number 1 on the planner's Top 20 Places "I Love to Visit" list. My manifestation is coming true because I am getting married on September 6, 2024, on Magic Island in Honolulu, Hawaii.

As I write the closing of my chapter today, I announced that I will be retiring on November 30, 2024, at the Leadership position in IT to allow myself to fully commit my time to my passion in life of helping others at my dream business *Lotus Soul Healing Arts, LLC*. I will devote my time to working with women who are ready to invest in improving their health by discovering the passion and purpose that fuels them to live the life of their dreams. Once they find the ultimate key to their passion, financial abundance will follow along with strong, healthy relationships.

About the Author

Diane Bovalino is a Usui/Holy Fire III online, World Peace, Karuna, and Usui/Tibetan Reiki Master, International Best-Selling Author, Intuitive Healer, Akashic Records Reader/Healer, Ama-Deus Practitioner, Crystal Healer, Registered Yoga Teacher, Passion and Purpose Coach, Reflexologist, and Brain Longevity Therapist.

Diane found her way back to health after being diagnosed with breast cancer. A now 17-year survivor, Diane says it is her passion and gift to share all the healing modalities she has learned since her diagnosis to change another life as these healing methods have saved her life.

Diane is here as a Light Worker to assist others on their healing journey back to their authentic self.

She holds a Master's Degree in Business Management and has invested 19 years in leadership positions. Diane coaches women one-on-one as a Passion & Purpose Coach. She has created a sacred container to work with women who are ready to turn their challenges in life into confidence and clarity to thrive and be empowered to live the life they deserve. Diane will work with them to find the "fire" in their life that has been missing. The key is that they will work together to manifest and create the life of their dreams.

Diane is the owner of *Lotus Soul Healing Arts, LLC,* a healing art center that is focused on assisting the individual on their personal healing journey. She focuses on working with each client who comes to the center as their specialized Intuitive Healer. All of Diane's healing sessions at *Lotus Soul Healing Arts* are tailored to each client, and all of the modalities she holds can be used in any session. Diane will intuitively channel in on each visit to define what the individual needs based on listening to the feedback given by the client, reading their chakras, bringing balance and healing through Reiki, Akashic Readings, Akashic Healings, Crystals, Ama-Deus Healings, Yoga, Yoga Nidra, Meditation, Spirituality classes, and Reflexology. Diane offers programs online, in-person, and even hybrid options.

You can sign up for a one-on-one Intuitive Discovery Session with Diane at no charge to identify actions for you to take to live the life you deserve and/or schedule a healing or coaching session with her at one of the links below.

Connect with Diane below:
- https://linktr.ee/Lotussoulhealingarts
- https://www.facebook.com/lotussoulhealingarts
- https://www.instagram.com/lotussoulhealingarts

GISELLE LORENA HURTADO

Pathways To Destiny

Shifting Higher Paths to Soul Purpose

On a cold night in Elko City, a bone-chilling winter storm swept through Juniper Street and 5th streets. The freezing landscape was breathtaking, with sub-zero temperatures, icy winds, and starry skies. The moon cast an otherworldly glow, evoking waves of nostalgia within me. Despite my eagerness to depart the city, I stared into the night and admired the bright, yellow moon and fiery stars framed by my window.

I'm going to miss this view so much. Moon gazing made a night like this "one" bittersweet. As I stared at the sparkling stars in the dark night sky, I was reminded that just as the stars once fulfilled their ancient purpose, so would I continue to fulfill mine. I picked up my bags, felt the weight of each step, and left. The soft click echoed behind me as I buried this moment into a memory. The spark that once lit my fire was abruptly extinguished, leaving my soul exposed, shallow, and shivering in the darkness of the night ahead.

The wind howled as I made my way to the alley at 3:33 a.m. I had my mini dachshund, one piece of luggage, and a carry-on waiting for my taxi. The storm's icy breath blew me side to side, but I gripped my train ticket and grounded myself against the old, scraped wooden pillar.

"Come on, where are you?" I whispered. I pulled my coat tighter and made my way to the end of the road, each step crunching deep into the snow. Part of me hoped the taxi wouldn't make it. Part of me was still holding on, and I felt my heart whither in hesitation. The suspense hung heavy as I peered into the darkness, straining to hear any sign of the approaching taxi. Every passing moment felt like an eternity, and the anticipation of the taxi's arrival brought nervousness and butterfly feelings – but not the warm and cozy ones.

Elko was beautiful yet cold that night, offering a change in the air as if I had stepped into a new frequency, shedding the weight of old, stagnant energy. My journey brought circumstantial clean-up, ego entanglements, and akashic karma at this time. Summoning the courage to leave the Ghost Town behind, I said goodbye to the illusion of being lost. Tonight, I'd be found whole and solemnly in my heart.

So, there I stood, resolute amid the turmoil, prepared for whatever came my way. In the midst of the storm, I saw through squinted eyes as a taxi approached slowly. The taxi driver arrived slightly late (around 3:35 a.m.) to pick us up and take us to the train station.

"Taxi for Giselle? The weather out here is crazy. Sorry, I'm late," the taxi driver apologized, giving me a sympathetic nod as he stopped.

I immediately snapped out of my deep thoughts and gathered my things. My breath was visible in the frosty air as I rushed to the trunk.

"Yes, that's me. Could you pop the trunk for me, please? It's freezing!" I replied, shivering. My cold hands fumbled with the door with hesitation, and for a moment, my heart sank. I opened the door and was greeted by warm air as I sat inside.

For the rest of the ride, there was little exchange of words, just small conversations about the weather and questions about my plans for Thanksgiving Day.

As I reached the train, I quickly made my way to the back of the line to board.

"Tickets, please!" the conductor requested. I boarded the train and sat in the back, feeling relieved yet uncertain. A tear slipped down my cheek as I leaned against the cold glass window, breaking the frost.

One luggage, starting from rock bottom, yet this time I felt different, less worried and more relieved. I silently prayed to myself and pondered my feelings. "God, lead me through this journey and make me stronger than ever. I have faith in your plans, and I know I'll be okay," I affirmed with trust. Destiny rises through us this way;

endings are just beginnings that always shine after darkness. I rode the train with trust and love, never looking back to my past.

My manifestation journey had just begun, and my next move was unclear to me at that time. I never expected this change would transform my soul and build a trusting relationship with the universe so I could be guided into my destiny. Manifestation is a relationship between oneself and the universe. It's a transformative journey of trust, faith, and releasing control, leading to a path of purpose and flow aligned with synchronicity. I was determined to become an author and a speaker to shed light on the Divine and elevate consciousness on Earth. I know that's why I'm here. With that mission, I'll do whatever it takes to follow my path – even taking chances and facing fears.

We have all had to start over at some point in life. I remember feeling back at square one with just a suitcase, trying to figure things out. But amidst the uncertainty, moments of magic and rebirth gave me hope.

I recently received news that filled me with excitement and shivers of anticipation. The news made me envision a future where I'm part of something extraordinary, working alongside others who have had their own transformative experiences. This would be the first time I officially became an author, another pull into my manifestation.

"Congratulations! You are officially an international best-selling author!" I read the text message that Katie Carey (this book's publisher) sent me with a screenshot of our previous collaboration,

"Evolving on Purpose: Co-creating with the Divine," listed as a #1 best seller on Amazon.

I can relate to the feeling of constant worry and self-doubt. It's like the universe was testing me at a time when everything seemed to be falling apart. I rewrote my chapter so many times because I felt like I wasn't good enough. It was a difficult time, but I refused to give up. Despite my hardships – financial difficulties, emotional struggles, and the fear of failure – I clung to my dream of being a published author. Writing my story tested my strength and resilience, and I was determined to prove myself. I diligently worked on myself mentally, physically, and emotionally, and slowly, opportunities started coming my way. It was almost as if the universe was waiting to see if I'd keep pushing forward. And I did. I've learned to see the world in a different light, and now, I'm eagerly waiting to see what the future holds.

The days were never short: meditation before sunrise, exercise, and a balanced breakfast. I made sure I got eight hours of sleep and eight hours of work. I wrote and read, meditated and enjoyed connecting with nature. Finally, my nights ended with gratitude, prayer, and reflection. This new chapter in my life was anything but dull. I reached a moment when I shifted from feeling like I had lost everything to realizing I already had everything I needed. I let go of control and aligned myself with love and creative energy, showing up for myself in ways I never had before. This mindset change brought many unexpected circumstances to guide me into my divinely synchronized path.

BECOMING THE MANIFESTING DIVA

For instance, in the next few months, I began to focus on my journey toward healing, gaining knowledge, and discovering unexpected opportunities for writing. I started noticing consecutive numbers appearing regularly. I found myself receiving random but helpful information. I felt guided by an inner voice, and messages channeled through me as I wrote. It all started with minor signs, like meeting a business mentor and author at a library who needed assistance writing his book. It felt like the right opportunity to pursue. Although nervous, this chance encounter led to me gaining a business mentor, a freelance writing job, and improved financial stability. It also boosted my confidence and helped me pursue my passion for writing. I trusted that my next step was already part of my journey, and as I thought, so I'd receive.

The release of my first book, Evolving on Purpose, marked a significant milestone in my life. Filled with pride and determination, I set up a table to sell copies, hoping to share my accomplishments with the world. However, despite my efforts, I didn't sell a single copy that day. I couldn't help but feel disheartened. Disappointed, I sought solace in my favorite spot near the river, where the gentle sunbeams illuminated the shallow waters beneath a bridge. There, I encountered an unexpected twist of fate that would alter my course. I was the one meant to receive a book from the universe that day.

To my surprise, I noticed three books placed deliberately beside me that were soaked from last night's rain: The Kybalion by Three Initiates, The Lost Keys of Masonry, and The Secret Teachings of All Ages by Manly P. Hall. Strangely, I had been yearning for guidance in the realm of ancient knowledge and healing just a few nights prior. I had prayed for divine intervention, allowing the universe to lead me towards enlightenment. Little did I know that the manifestation of my deepest desires was unfolding before me at that very moment. It was as if these books had beckoned to me, drawing me closer to their wisdom. What's more astonishing, I realized that I was sitting in front of the Masonic building at the time, an odd synchronicity that sent shivers down my spine.

As the days unfolded, I found myself immersed in a series of otherworldly encounters. Messages from the Divine seemed to reach me through unexpected avenues – from mysterious meditations playing on my phone to the uncanny proximity of animals and butterflies. It was as though the universe was whispering secrets into my ears, guiding me towards my destiny.

Intrigued by these events, I turned to tarot readings to explore the depths of my spiritual realm and intuition. These readings unveiled prophetic visions and dreams, rendering me awestruck by their accuracy. I discovered that my innate gift of visualization allowed me to tap into my energy and sometimes the energy of others, granting me profound insights and images. In a deep meditation, I received insight into my past that I had been a shaman. I was a natural-born healer in past lifetimes. I took this information and began to study energy work, and I had already been doing herbalism for some time. Naturally, I was already following my path.

My intuition and abilities burgeoned in the following months, unveiling a seamless connection between myself, God, and the universe. Every moment felt like a divine revelation, as if the cosmos conspired to bring me closer to my soul purpose.

The most enthralling aspect of this journey was the concept of "downloads" – moments when the universe granted me visions during meditation and wisdom. As I became more harmonious within myself, the messages from my spirit guides grew louder and more apparent, flooding my soul with enlightenment. I began to comprehend that manifestation isn't merely a stroke of luck but a harmonious alignment within the cosmic energy system, an omnipotent force that resides within each of us.

When you trust in the creative source and let go of "hows," "whens," and "what-ifs," the things you desire begin to magnetize toward you. You signal to the universe that you're ready to receive all that's meant for you. Manifestations are the physical reality of your meaning – the highest version of yourself in alignment with your purpose. Your creations, passions, and willpower will take you there.

Hardships teach you to evolve into oneness with yourself, the universe, and the creative source. Your painful journey will reflect resilience, trust in the universe, and faith. Use this as a weapon to overcome darkness. To become all you want, you must be comfortable with the opposite. For example, silence makes you feel alone, but also makes you closer to yourself and Source.

Exercising makes you feel weak, but it actually makes you stronger. In this way, manifestation is your will to take action toward your dream. If you feel uncomfortable, good! You're supposed to feel uncomfortable in order to experience profound transformation. Just as a butterfly must feel uncomfortable in a cocoon before finally breaking free, eventually, your struggles will turn into your strengths.

If you want to expand your magnetic scale, spiritual evolution, and connection to source, I will share my top six strategies that I know will inspire you to embrace your own transformational paths. Together, let's bridge the gap between you, the universe, and your heart. You can call back your power in manifesting... now!

1. Set a Pure Intention

Intention lights up your path and fuels your determination. Intentions serve as anchors in the present moment and are deeply connected to our virtues and the person we strive to be every day. Whether it's compassion, kindness, or honesty, intention helps you embody the mindset and behaviors of the person you aspire to be. Moreover, when your intention comes from a pure heart, its driving force amplifies, making it even more powerful and attractive. Your intention serves as a magnetic force. Including God in your desires, thoughts, and heart can elevate your intentions to a higher level. When your heart is pure, and your actions align with your purpose, you open yourself up to a cascade of flowing, positive energy.

Focus on the person you are *being* – not on the activities you are doing. Ask yourself, "How do I want to be today?" Envision the kind of person you aspire to be and consider the actions you can take to embody that person. Start your day by setting your intention instead of diving into your to-do list. You might need to make changes to your daily routine to align with this intention. Keeping a journal of your intentions or creating affirmations can help you incorporate this practice into your daily life.

Remember to reflect on your day before going to bed. Think about everything you did from the start of the morning to the end of the day. Consider whether you're satisfied with how you spent your day. Did you stick to your intentions? This kind of reflection can reset your subconscious by making you aware of and reflecting on your actions. By doing so, you can change the way daily events affect your future self.

2. Cultivate Gratitude

Gratitude is a powerful energy that connects us to the universe and our creator. When we truly feel grateful, it triggers the release of chemicals like serotonin and dopamine in our bodies, making us feel happier and more at peace. The key is to turn grateful thoughts into deep, heartfelt feelings. By expressing gratitude to our ancestors, nature, other people, and the creative source, we can tune into a higher frequency of positivity. Embracing gratitude can shift our perspectives, uplifting our mood and behavior.

Gratitude is not just an occasional act but a way of life. Prayer is another powerful way to connect with the Great Spirit and be thankful – even for the smallest things, like the first breath in the morning or a daily meal. Practicing gratitude enhances our overall way of being, making us more magnetic and attuned to positivity.

If you want to reach a relaxed state of mind and be more present, try this quick 5-10-minute meditation daily. Start by practicing slow, deep breathing – inhale for five seconds, hold for 5 seconds, then exhale for five seconds and hold for five seconds. This is called "box breathing." As you do this, place your hand on your heart and focus on positive emotions like joy and compassion. Imagine yourself living the life you desire and feeling those positive emotions as if they're already true. You draw awareness to its energy by touching and connecting with your heart. Be grateful for experiencing those positive emotions, and trust that they will come into your life soon.

3. Build Fortitude

Don't be afraid to walk through the valley of pain. Fortitude means having the strength and resilience to overcome challenges. Step out of your comfort zone and start improving in every part of your life. Remember, everything has a yin and a yang. Find your duality and accept the darkness. You wouldn't be who you are today without it.

As you start your day, think of ways to introduce voluntary discomfort. Some ways could be a cold shower, skipping coffee, fasting, exercising, or meditating on a painful experience. These daily acts train the mind and spirit to be resilient, preparing you for future challenges. We'll never grow if we don't get comfortable with feeling uncomfortable. If you don't give yourself opportunities to experience some pain and discomfort, the universe will do it for you.

Practice *amor fati* in your daily life. *Amor fati* is a practice rooted in stoicism, which involves loving one's destiny, whether it brings joy or sorrow. The stoic individual endures pain or hardships without complaint, refusing to succumb to emotional tyranny. This practice encourages you to embrace your fate, whatever it may be. It's a passionate acceptance of whatever life serves you, be it sorrow, triumph, or tribulation. Each day presents us with a mystery. Practice being open to whatever life brings your way.

4. Trust the Universe and Let Go

Your expectations limit your results; let them go. See the multidimensional energy behind the unknown, embrace it, and double it. Release yourself from the set of rules you put around money and life. Release the attachments to the required actions needed to reach your dreams. Release the doubt about how your dreams will come or happen. Openly trusting the universe will bring forward what's meant for you and attract a life that aligns with your highest self. Don't trap the magic of universal forces in specifications or enclosed outcomes to your manifestations. So much 'soul planning' is going on for us beyond the veil.

As we tap into our strengths and strive to unite with the divine energy and flow, our attention turns towards cultivating inner peace and freedom. Along our journey, infinite possibilities await us, and attempting to control what unfolds limits our potential. The outcome is beyond our control. Not knowing the future is similar to loving, trusting, and letting go. If we impose our will upon our desires or outcomes, we signal to the universe that we rely on control to protect ourselves. This control indicates a lack of trust in the plans for our greater good. Let yourself be guided; there is nothing to hold on to, and the potential of your vibration is quantum, infinite. Rules of time and control don't apply in the quantum world. Whether you believe in God or a higher power, remember your origin is infinite energy, and the truth of your path will reveal itself as you begin to live in the present moment and fulfill your soul with love.

5. Visualize

Visualization is a staple of spiritual practice for a maturing, evolving soul like yourself. Acknowledging that you are a part of the divine system and allowing your visualizations to flow freely will bring forward images of your past lives, information about your soul's path, prophetic dreams, and your true heart's desire.

Pleasant imagery can also be incredibly healing and relax the heart and mind. If you see yourself doing something in your mind, visualization can help bring that to life. The visualization journey is unique to you and moves you deeper into the unknown realm of Spirit. Be ready to see images of things you cannot understand just yet. Call upon the free flow of Spirit and journey within. Visualization is a tool used for many years in shamanism.

"The Gateway Experience" is a powerful asset to your meditation life. Go on a journey in your meditation and visualize traveling to planets, visiting your past lives, or people who await you on the other side. Let your mind take you on a journey. Visualize this experience, and don't hold any attachments to it. You can find the complete experience on YouTube called "The Gateway Experience."

BECOMING THE MANIFESTING DIVA

6. Practice The Law of Resonance

To physically manifest your desired reality, you must reach resonance with the vibration of your desired life. Everything in the universe is energy, requiring resonance to tune into an aligned frequency. Resonance is the echo of your vibration, and what we receive back is not what we desire but who we are. You are the reflection of the vibration you put out into the web of the cosmos. Therefore, our vibration is why we can be dissatisfied with what we attract. We adjust our thoughts and actions to attract our dreams; however, without becoming the vibration of that higher being, we cannot expect to be reciprocated with outcomes of a higher power! Remember, you don't "want" your dreams; you ARE your dreams.

Resonance governs our entire experiences, and much like tuning forks resonate through an exchange of frequency, we can bring our physical and energy bodies to resonate with each other. Focus on refining each frequency within your physical, mental, emotional, and spiritual bodies. Practice working on each of these and create a subconscious habit of feeling in tune with all energy bodies.

The mental body can hold cognitive dissonance, which means experiencing mental discomfort when confronting conflicting beliefs, values, and ideas. This can disturb our resonance and ability to connect. Create a mental space to accept new information with an open mind. Don't engage in internal conflicts or contradictions. Embracing others' thoughts or opposing beliefs allows a pure, calm mind to arise, enabling you to escape the low vibrations of anger, fear, sadness, and doubt.

Through my journey of ascension, I've grappled with the fear of failure and judgment. It's been quite a transformation from who I used to be. Before reaching for greatness, I had to confront that I had been attracting darkness into my life for a long time. I had to let go of a lot to gain; I had to endure pain to understand love and embrace trust without certainty. I'm still a work in progress, continuously working on myself and my manifestations. This journey brings exploration and an abundance of love, unwavering trust in God, the universe, and yourself.

To all the manifesting queens out there, it's a genuine honor to connect with every soul. I extend my best wishes to you on your divine pursuits and send infinite blessings.

And so it is.

About the Author

G*iselle Lorena Hurtado* has evolved from a time of darkness into an advocate for spreading messages of love, light, and self-mastery. Giselle guides others in processing their experiences and moving from trauma to healing. Amid chaotic situations and having a passion for writing, she has moved forward with a desire to teach others about the Divine within us. She has dedicated seven years to practices such as energy body healing, meditations, and spiritual self-awareness. Her knowledge expands to ancient hermetic teachings, universal principles of law, and esotericism.

Giselle's mission is to help others connect with their inner masters, teachers, and ancestors to embrace their light, love, and compassion. She believes if we look further into our thoughts and state of consciousness, we can raise our emotional intelligence and bring awareness to necessary inner healing.

Giselle Hurtado is also an International Best-Selling Author of *Evolving on Purpose: Co-creating with the Divine*, an herbalist, and a spiritual enthusiast who shares the wisdom of our divinity. From darkness to a life of light and love, she continues to learn and create transformational guidance to help seed a new generation of transcendence.

Connect with Giselle below:

- https://www.facebook.com/jennifer.lorena.7

JO-ANNE ROSS

Return to Wholeness

Lyme Disease is a bitch! There. I said it. This nasty disease stole seven years of my life. Seven years spent in constant misery and pain. Years, where, at times, I didn't even want to be here among the living anymore.

Step by step, day by day, increment by increment that changed.

Today, I LOVE my life! I say this every single day. Some days, I sing it while dancing with my cats. Some days, I shout it out loud in the shower. Some days I whisper it quietly to myself. I say it with a heart full of gratitude, love, and joy. My life is amazing, and I know my life will only keep getting bigger and greater, for I am a *Super Manifesting Diva*.

You must be wondering how I got from unrelenting misery and pain to a life of joy and abundance. Well, let me tell you the story.

Once upon a time, there was a little girl named Jo-Anne who seemed to live an idyllic life – a loving family, middle-class upbringing, friends, intelligence, and health. What more could a girl possibly ask for?

Well, in retrospect, it appears I could have asked for a little more emotional intelligence and a better understanding of my gut and it's messages.

Now, decades later, with a lifetime of wisdom and knowledge, I can look back and see that this beautiful childhood was filled with tiny moments of loving teasing by Family members and moments that I twisted around in my head and misinterpreted in my own unique way. As a child, I did not understand that teasing me was the way that some people showed their love for me. Asking me where the other 2% was when I had gotten 98% on a math test was their way of saying *"Wow that is so close to a perfect score"*, and not *"What is wrong with you? You only needed two more points to be perfect"*. Add in a generous sprinkling of generational wounds, mix, and *voila*! Little Jo-Anne morphed into a woman driven by perfectionism and people-pleasing.

During adulthood, the Universe sent me sign after sign, message after message—"Hey girly, wake up! This is not right!

BECOMING THE MANIFESTING DIVA

DANGER! DANGER! Run away!" The signs and messages were frequent and diverse—celebration venues booked for special occasions went bankrupt, appointments canceled, broken promises, blatant lies, unexplained computer glitches...Because I spent so many years ignoring these signs and messages, I learned to be incredibly brave, strong, resilient, and independent to get through my struggles and trauma.

As it turns out, these traits saved my life, but at the time, the majority of the Universe's signs and messages went largely unnoticed, and all that were noticed were certainly dismissed and ignored.

That is, until one day, when the signs and messages could no longer be ignored. The Universe sent me its big guns! Agent Illness came knocking. And this time, I couldn't hide behind closed doors and say, *"No, thanks! I already gave at the office."* Agent Illness brutally burst down the door, kidnapped me, and held me hostage for seven long years until I learned the many, many, many lessons they had to teach me. I continue and will continue to learn on a daily basis, but I can safely say, Agent Illness finally set me free.

Here is the story of where the illness first made itself known and where the lessons began. On a lovely summer's day, my Son, my Boyfriend, and I were in the garage working on changing the motor in his car – you know, normal Mother Son stuff. I squatted down like I had a million times before to pick up a tool, but this time was not like those other million times before. Actually, it was like never before. My left knee stopped me mid-squat.

"What the heck?"

I got up and tried again, but the result was the same. We kept working, but I could only think, *"What was that all about?"*

I continued to suffer, and my swollen, sore knee became so much worse and morphed into so much more.

I kept thinking to myself, *"Do I have Lyme Disease? What if this is the West Nile Virus?"*

I went to the doctor and was tested for both. Both tests came back negative. *"Whew, thank Heavens!"*

Prior to June 2013, I was an extremely active athlete. I regularly participated in a wide array of exercises and physical activities: weight training, swimming, women's hockey, softball, yoga, kickboxing, Zumba, soccer, street hockey, ultimate frisbee, water skiing, hiking in the mountains in Arizona, rollerblading, bicycling, and repairs and maintenance around the house (I was strong enough to carry a bundle of shingles up a ladder).

Then suddenly, daily tasks such as getting out of bed, brushing my teeth, showering, cutting my food, climbing stairs one at a time, going down the stairs backwards one step at a time, getting in and out of a vehicle, walking any distance (with a limp, slow and labored), rolling over in bed, combing my hair, even getting dressed became exhausting and depleting.

I was in constant pain. I spent 24 hours a day trying to find a comfortable position. I could only sit, stand, move around, or lie down for short periods at a time. I was foggy-headed, confused, suffered memory loss, was unable to concentrate, and had difficulty coming up with words. Malaise and nausea were seldom far from my side. I was often hit with the need to lie down – immediately. No matter where I was or what I was doing, I absolutely had to lie down NOW.

Over time, every single system in my body was affected – including my personality. I went from being energetic, optimistic, and extroverted to sullen, depressed and introverted.

As if being chronically sick was not enough, I had lost … well… everything. I was no longer able to work, so I was no longer an employee, Chartered Professional Accountant, or Certified Internal Auditor. I was no longer a hockey player, swimmer, hiker, skater, landscaper, motorcyclist, skier, soccer player, or baseball player. I had lost my beautiful, well-toned muscles.

My young adult and teenage Children were living mostly with their Father. My Boyfriend was living overseas working as a contractor in Saudi Arabia. I was even too weak to hold my brand-new Granddaughter on my own, and the occasional sleepovers with her disappeared. I was broken and alone. I was in mourning. I was grieving the death of all I cherished in my life.

For years—yes, years—I went to doctor after doctor, specialist after specialist, hundreds of appointments, X-rays, MRIs, scans, tests, tests, and more tests—all with the same result: *"You are a mystery."*

There were definite markers in my blood of swelling and crisis, but no definitive answer. I was getting sicker and sicker and weaker and weaker. My poor Dad was so scared that I was going to die, and if things had not changed when they did, his fears would likely have been realized in short order.

Still, Lyme Disease kept playing in my head over and over. This time, I listened to my gut. I started researching Lyme Disease on my own. From what I could tell, Lyme Disease was a perfect match for my ever-changing, mysterious body-wide symptoms. They even call Lyme Disease "the Great Imitator," as it mimics the symptoms of so many other diseases.

I finally went to see a Naturopath and paid to have my blood work sent out of the country for testing. The results came back very definite – Lyme Disease! I wasn't crazy! I had been right all along! Thank you, gut! I heard you, and I finally listened to you!

A few years later, I was tested again, using a different testing protocol conducted in yet another country. Once again, the results came back with a definite answer: Lyme Disease (along with Babesia, Bartonella, and walking Pneumonia). Finally, I had an answer and could start making my very long journey back to health.

The journey back to myself—my true self—has been a long one. It has had many twists and turns. It has required that I make so many changes in how I think, how I act, what I believe, and how I am. The discoveries I have made along the way have been awe-inspiring, enlightening, and oftentimes fun! I was back to my rose-coloured glasses, silver linings, and the glass three-quarters full outlook on life.

BECOMING THE MANIFESTING DIVA

In my initial interview with my naturopathic doctor, he asked, *"Did you have a stressful event about a month before you first noticed the symptoms?"*

"YES!" When I went back home and looked at my calendar, it was almost a month to the day between a HUGE stressful event of a trusted Friend being incredibly cruel and the onslaught of my symptoms.

This was **LESSON ONE: Mind-Body Connection**

If ignored, eventually, chronic stress leads to illness and disease.

This same naturopathic doctor administered my 10 Pass Ozone Therapy treatments – yup, that's right! I had blood drawn out of my arm, filled with ozone, and pumped back into my arm – not once, not twice, but 10 times in a single sitting.

I was terrified at first, but I trusted my Naturopath and the research I had done. And at this point, I was willing to try just about anything to get better. I incorporated naturopathic medicine and Eastern healing methodologies into my rehabilitation. I did hypnosis, acupuncture, tapping, chiropractic work, massage therapy, flotation therapy, yoga, meditation, tai chi… and eventually, it worked!

During one of these ozone treatments, my Naturopath casually shared with me about an experience he had with his Sister in a reading with a local medium. As a doctor and a scientist, he was initially very skeptical, but he walked away from the meeting transformed.

I have always been fascinated by mediums. Because of my casual chat with my Naturopath, I contacted the medium he had visited, and she agreed to work with me. I had always thought only the rich and famous would have the privilege of working with a medium – something so outside my realm of possibility. Now, I have a dozen friends who are mediums! What are the chances? Oh, wait… can you say *manifestation*?

My experience with the medium opened my eyes. Some things I experienced dovetail beautifully with my religious upbringing. And then, so much more beyond that. I connected with Family members who had passed and who, during the reading, shared stories of our life together, shared things that had happened in my life since their passing, and they let me know how much they loved me. I learned to appreciate the beauty of the afterlife. How our loved ones who have passed are always with us, watching over us, accessible to us at any time. We can talk to them: anytime, anywhere. We can ask them, our Angels, or the Divine for help. They are not to be feared. And when we ask, they do help us. It may not always work out the way we envisioned. Our life's circumstances are intended to help our soul learn and grow. The journey may not always be an easy journey, but sometimes that is what we need to pay attention and learn our life lessons. To return to wholeness and live bigger and better lives.

Because of this lovely medium, I can proudly say, "*I am the hand of the Divine*". There is no grandiosity in that statement. It is just a statement of fact. I am so much more than the human being that I am right now. And I am enough. In fact, I am perfect – just the way I am in this very moment.

This was **LESSON TWO: Spirituality is so much more than religion**

Being on long-term disability, my full-time job was to get better, so I could get back to work. Since exercise had always been such a huge part of my life, exercise had to eventually make its way back into my life. So, I started with yoga.

Now, let's be clear: although I took advantage of yoga classes offered at my workplace, yoga was not my thing. I thought yoga was for sedentary people. I was more of a kickboxing kind of girl, but a body has to start somewhere.

At first, I spent the entire class forcing my body to move, pulling with my arms to roll over, struggling to stand, and then lying back down on my mat.

That was it.

That was the entire class.

I got down on the mat and then made my way back to standing once or twice during the entire hour class. After several weeks, it got a little better – literally one small step at a time. Now, I am a yoga instructor for adults, children, and teens.

This was **LESSON THREE: Do not Judge**

Be discerning in what is right for you, and be open to try new things. Yoga is so much more than a few poses. It is a philosophy, a way of life. Some of the basic teachings in yoga are that you are a whole – not just a mind and a separate body and spirit. You are the whole package. Studying Patanjali, a scholar from the 5th century BC, taught me so much. Patanjali says the practice of yoga helps us remove the symptoms and causes of our physical and mental problems and discover our inner being. Through the teachings of the mastery of the mind, I learned that our perception of our reality impacts everything. I learned to be present in the moment. Yoga taught me to be true to myself and good to myself. It also reinforced being good to society, the planet, and the universe. I am a Yogini through and through.

Earlier on in my adulthood, I had attended some group counseling sessions. In the beginning, I would sit quietly, and if someone asked, "*How are you?*" I would quickly reply, "*I'm fine.*"

I was existing safely behind the wall I had so carefully constructed, brick by brick. I was shielding myself from the trauma of my home life.

"*Your words can't touch me. You can't hurt me. I am safe here.*"

After listening to so many others share week after week, something breached my brick wall and created a crack. My wall started to crumble, and all my emotions came barreling through like Niagara Falls. I cried and cried and cried.

BECOMING THE MANIFESTING DIVA

With the gift of hindsight, I can see how my bottled-up, repressed emotions had led to my prior brushes with Agent Illness. Agent Illness and I had danced for some time. I did a little work to heal myself, but never really learned all my lessons until decades later.

This was **LESSON FOUR: Emotions are messages that should never be ignored**

We must learn to feel our emotions, label them, understand them, and mindfully find healthy ways to work through them. What are your emotions trying to communicate to you? Repressing them, drinking them, burying them, eating them, snorting them, porning them, shopping them… away never works. Ignoring them impacts your body and, if left to fester, will eventually lead to illness or disease.

While in recovery, I took more time to notice all that was going on around me. So many kids and teens were suffering from stress, anxiety and overwhelm. The number of children and teens as young as six who were taking their own lives was alarming to me. And I couldn't help but wonder about the experience of being a kid today. Nothing is taboo. Nothing is sacred. Children are shielded from nothing. They hold everything – both the beauty and the ugliness of this world – in the palm of their hands.

How can a little developing brain comprehend what they are seeing and the longer-term ramifications of war, murder, cruelty, pornography? Where is innocence, free play, and abandonment that comes with being a child?

My heart ached.

I decided to learn how to help kids and teens navigate this fast-paced, confusing, and oftentimes terrifying world. I signed up to become a Meditation Tutor for Kids and Teens with and without Autism, ADHD, Trauma, and Special Education Needs. I loved it, and I became a Certified Meditation Tutor!

Lorraine Murphy, the CEO of the meditation school Connected Kids TM, posted about an experiment she was joining. It was $25 US for a whole year. The deadline was midnight December 31st, and I couldn't decide whether to join. I was off work and broke. Was I willing to spend another $25… in US funds?!? The social media posts kept coming up over and over. Finally, at 11:59 pm, December 31st, I enrolled. I signed up for the Million Dollar Experiment with Joanna Hunter. Well, let me tell you, this was one of the best decisions of my life! The Universe led me to this place and time with the opportunity to participate in this experiment. Free will was mine. The decision was mine. Do I sign up, or don't I? Synchronicity brought me here, and my nagging gut helped me decide.

This was **LESSON FIVE: Listen to your Gut. It never lies**

The Universe is constantly sending you information: signs, symbols, and synchronicities which hold the power to heal you. The Divine, your Soul, your Soul Family, your Angels, Guides, and those who have gone before you send you messages. Listen for them.

BECOMING THE MANIFESTING DIVA

Listen to them. They are *Letters from Home* telling you how much you are loved and cared for. Always.

Joanna Hunter became my mentor, coach, and friend. She is the one who led me to the beautiful and talented Katie Carey (the publisher of this book). Through Joanna's teachings and her recommended books and authors, I became a LightWeb® Priestess and learned so much about Heaven and Earth and what it means to have this human experience.

These were LESSONS SIX, SEVEN, EIGHT… to INFINITY and BEYOND, Beyond, beyond…

We are bound by our limiting beliefs, which impact every thought we think, decision we make, and action we take. On the positive side, we have the ability to change these beliefs. Did you know everything is vibration? Including your thoughts? Including your emotions – energy in motion! You have the ability to change your vibration with your thoughts, and because energy and vibration attracts similar energy and vibration like a big old magnet, more positive energy and vibration attracts more positive… everything!

And, of course, there were lessons in spirituality. Joanna is also a medium who channels a team from the spiritual realm. The multitude of lessons she taught me in spirituality were life-altering. I learned about downloads, channeling, akashic records, auras, our connection to spirit, the duality of Source and Void and so much more.

The new interests that Joanna sparked in me led me to the Real Success Summit, where I wanted to listen to Deepak Chopra. There I was, introduced to a whole other world – Les Brown, Forbes Riley, Kane and Alessia Minkus, Jack Canfield, Richard Harrington, Sharon Lechter, Grant Cardone, Paul O'Mahony, and John Lee.

I was captivated. There was so much to learn and new ways to think. I eventually signed up to work with Kane and Alessia Minkus and volunteered at one of their events, where I had the opportunity to meet all the presenters and get to know them. This opened the door to working events with James MacNeil and then with Robin Banks, where I met four incredible souls who are definitely part of my Soul Family. This path led me to work with Raul Lopez Jr. and Brandon Hintz and be on the virtual stage with the incredible Les Brown, as well as being a co-author in one of Les Brown's books. Let me say that again: *Les Brown!*

My wonderful and crazy journey then led me to work with the powerhouse Forbes Riley. Whoa! While working with her, I met more incredible souls who are also definitely part of my Soul Family. Can you believe it? Little ol' me working with these famous and well-respected people!

Say it with me:

M-A-N-I-F-E-S-T-A-T-I-O-N!

Some of these incredible people, their families, and their staff have become dear friends who have changed my life. I LOVE MY

BECOMING THE MANIFESTING DIVA

LIFE! I consider some of these incredible humans part of my family—people who are instrumental in my manifestations and my impact on this world.

There were many dark years when I did the best I could with the tools and knowledge I had available. At the time, I didn't know what I didn't know. Now, with the knowledge and wisdom that I have today, I know that I caused trauma for my kids, and for that, I am deeply sorry.

If I had only known better… I love my beautiful children with all my heart and worked very hard to give them an amazing, loving, and fun-filled childhood. I wasn't perfect, but then, none of us are. It is part of being human.

We all have lessons to learn to become the people we were meant to be. We all have experiences that we need to go through to learn these lessons. Some of us are quick learners, and some of us are not. Other mitigating circumstances always come into play that you have to learn to maneuver around and work with.

Now, I love to teach others in my circle of friends, in my Family, in my Granddaughter's school, and in my business. I love it when people tell me they hear my voice in their head, or they tell me, *"I wish Jo-Anne was here. She'd coach us on what to do,"* or *"Jo-Anne would remind me that I have the right to say, 'No, that doesn't work for me!'"*

My time is now spent speaking, developing, and offering programs and coaching for families and caregivers of those touched by Dementia. I am also working on developing my Dementia Village and Wellness Community: *Chez Juliette*. I am proud to be known as the "Dementia with Dignity Champion!"

Through a fun, engaging, and inspiring community, my goal is to change the landscape of care for Dementia residents, their Families, and their caregivers. Only when we are whole and healthy ourselves, can we effectively care for others.

My programs teach the ME FIRST method to get back to the wholeness we were born with and encompass emotional, mental, physical, and spiritual health. We address the science and influence of limiting beliefs, emotions, childhood trauma, yoga philosophy, meditation, Emotional Freedom Technique (EFT), mind-body connection, the power of the mind, spirituality and the science of menopausal health, as many caregivers for Dementia relatives are menopausal women.

Chez Juliette is named in honour of my beautiful Mom, who suffered from Dementia for over ten years. I lived with her for nine months and was her primary caregiver. Although I no longer lived with her over the following years, I continued to be one of her caregivers. I witnessed firsthand how this disease affects not only the person afflicted but also all those around them.

Chez Juliette, my programs, coaching, speaking engagements, and upcoming book (A Dementia Survival Guide for Families and Caregivers) will encompass much of what I have learned over the last several years about what is needed to have quality of life and to live with dignity, fun, and harmony with our true selves.

BECOMING THE MANIFESTING DIVA

Oh, and in case you were wondering my greatest manifestation… Me! I love the me that I am today! It took me a long time and a lot of hard work to get here, but I always knew the kind of person I was meant to be. All the hard work and suffering of the past was well worth the me I am today.

About the Author

Jo-Anne Ross, from Savour the Moment in Serenity, is a multifaceted individual. She is a speaker, teacher, coach, and an author. Jo-Anne possesses a unique blend of skills, experience, and expertise in both the business and wellness domains.

Throughout her professional career, she served as a Chartered Public Accountant and Certified Internal Auditor. These years of experience allowed her to develop robust interpersonal, problem-solving, and communication skills. She took great pleasure in researching best practices and formulating recommendations to enhance business systems for her clients.

In the past decade, Jo-Anne has expanded her horizons by earning certifications as a Meditation Tutor and Yoga Instructor. She has complemented these certifications with training in the Emotional Freedom Technique and extensive studies in Emotional Intelligence and the mind-body connection. Currently, she is pursuing advanced studies with Dr. Stacy T. Sims, focusing on the science of menopause.

Jo-Anne spent 9 months living with her Mom as her sole caregiver through her Mom's struggles through the early stages of Dementia. In the years that followed, Jo-Anne's experiences with her Mom lit a burning desire for change. She has designed the first franchisable Dementia Village and Wellness Community and is currently working on her book, which will be... *A Dementia Survival Guide for Families and Caregivers.*

Jo-Anne's dedication lies in providing enriching programs and coaching for the Families and Caregivers of Dementia sufferers. She is known as the *Dementia with Dignity Champion.* Her goal is to guide us back to the wholeness we were born with, using her ME FIRST system, encompassing emotional, mental, physical, and spiritual aspects. Jo-Anne teaches and coaches on a range of topics, including the science and influence of limiting beliefs, emotions, childhood trauma, yoga philosophy, meditation, Emotional Freedom Technique, mind-body connection and the science of menopause.

Her true passion lies in creating fun, engaging, and nurturing environments that facilitate growth, self-love, and transformation. Through her distinct amalgamation of expertise, Jo-Anne Ross continues to inspire and empower individuals on their journey toward self-discovery, success, and their journey back to wholeness. Jo-Anne is proud to guide you to your best self, healed and prepared to offer compassionate care to others.

Connect with Jo-Anne Ross below:

- https://www.savourthemomentinserenity.ca/
- https://www.instagram.com/savourthemomentinserenity/
- https://www.facebook.com/SavourTheMomentinSerenity

KARLA KOPP

Creating Dreams Come True

My Dreams are coming true! It's too exciting not to share. Maybe sharing makes it more real? Sharing my dreams certainly makes things more FUN!

I want to share my dream and my story with you in hopes of helping you realize your dreams and allowing them to expand – rather than resisting them – the way many of us have been taught.

Sometimes, in my sharing, people respond with "WOW! I could never do that because…" or "I'd like to do that BUT…" How often have those kinds of excuses popped up in your life? I've had plenty of them!

BECOMING THE MANIFESTING DIVA

After my first cruise in 1993, I've held on to one particular dream: "When I retire, I want to live on a cruise ship!" This dream has never had any doubts, worries, or fears attached to it. I happily shared it with others over the years with confidence, and they would often ask questions about how that would work. Their doubtful questions never bothered me. In fact, they inspired me to find those answers and to get prepared!

This wasn't my "norm." Usually, when making decisions, I ask myself a million questions. I get lost in a sea of "what ifs," and I wonder how things will work out. Those worries and fears keep me from moving forward towards my desires.

When we stay stuck in the "how," we believe that what we want is way over there, far away, unreachable. We can't get "over there" from here. It's like a flat tire. We could fret and complain that our tire is flat, and we can't go anywhere now, or we can get the tools from the trunk and change the tire!

I will share several tools that have been important in changing my way of thinking. My journey into self-discovery began several years ago with Louise L Hay who has changed many lives with her belief that there is only one thing that solves all problems and that is: "To Love Yourself". Louise is the author of multiple resources for learning to love yourself including books, card decks, audio/CD programs and calendars. I've gathered so many tools from so many different mentors like Louise who spread the word of self-love. "Abraham"- Esther Hicks is an inspirational speaker, channeler, and author who believes that 'Your thoughts create what happens in the physical world". They teach that you are a powerful creator who can use your thoughts to create whatever you want in the physical world". Mike Dooley is a New York Times best-selling author, speaker and entrepreneur who teaches "Thoughts become Things". Mary Morrisey created Dream Builders, a coaching program that gives support and tools needed to create your dream life.

Whenever you are feeling less than good, if you will stop and say:

'Nothing is more important than that I feel good.
I want to find a reason NOW to feel good,'
you will find an improved thought." ~ Abraham Hicks

One key point Abraham makes is that our goal is to feel good. Sounds simple, right? If I feel good, I'll have what I want! Then comes that flat tire, the sore throat, a cough, and the angry people in traffic. Let's face it: it doesn't always feel easy to feel good!

I've noticed that as contrast shows up, I may find myself on that roller coaster of feelings of fear, worry, and doubt. I soon become more distressed by the worrisome feelings than the actual contrast! Noticing my worries and doubts helps me turn my thoughts towards what I desire and what I can do right now in this circumstance. Perhaps I need to accept and allow the contrast and ask: "What is telling/teaching me right now.

A recent example of contrast for me has been in my health. I had an eardrum rupture which caused hearing loss and vestibular damage in my ears, affecting my balance. My initial reaction was fear.

BECOMING THE MANIFESTING DIVA

Fear of losing my independence. As I've navigated through doctor appointments, vestibular therapy, and other helpful services, I've come to realize what this is teaching me.

I'm learning to slow down, not be in such a rush to do everything at once, relax, and enjoy all the incredible blessings I have. As I slow down, I'm listening within. I'm listening to myself, to what my soul is expressing. I actually love the quiet most of the time; it calms my body and spirit. I've taken up coloring again, which is so peaceful and calming.

It's interesting that I've always said I have better balance on a ship than on land. I've been on three cruises since the rupture, and I'm fine on the ship. It feels like my inner being is absolutely taking care of me!

"Thoughts become things." ~ Mike Dooley

What would help me feel better right now? Mike Dooley says: "Thoughts become things." I can often track contrast back to negative, worrisome thoughts. In this recent contrast, doctors were first on the list. My vestibular therapy therapist was amazing and taught me so much about balance, movement, and exercises that I can continue to keep my balance in check.

I also had appointments with my chiropractor for back issues (which are important in the alignment of the body), and I see my massage therapist weekly. I'm giving my body everything possible to improve my health and fitness. I can no longer go to 9Round kickboxing, but I can do other forms of exercise along with daily walking.

Healing my body, mind, and soul has become a top priority, and with the other tools listed below, I am confident in continuing towards my dreams of cruising around the world!

> *"It's easy to feel good. It is easy.*
> *It is easy to create your own reality.*
> *It is easy to think a thought you choose to think.*
> *It is easy to feel better than you feel right now."*
> ~Abraham Hicks

My current favorite high-flying disc thoughts are imagining the fun of my next cruises I have scheduled. Recently, I had a World Cruise planned, and everything fell through. I began to look for another cruise with the thought that second on my bucket list of locations to visit is Australia and New Zealand, which were both going to be on the World Cruise. I found a much better itinerary for Australia and New Zealand which will have a much richer experience!

This is a great example of something not working out, and it's replaced by something even better that gets me back in sync with what I desire and feeling so much better. Feeling better and feeling amazing is our ultimate goal! To Live! Laugh! Love! And Learn! Not only do I feel better, but I also make better decisions and create more of what I love. I create the life I love!

BECOMING THE MANIFESTING DIVA

"What we think, we become." ~ Buddha

Besides my strong desire to feel better, I now have several tools in place:

Mentors. As mentioned, I have several wonderful mentors with whom I keep in touch through quotes, books, YouTube, Facebook groups, weekly Zoom sessions, and many other ways.

Grounding and Meditation. Getting out of the mind chatter that wants to worry about everything and moving into my heart space.

Gratitude. Appreciation on a daily, moment by moment basis. I express appreciation upon waking up each morning; before I go to sleep at night I write in my journal of appreciation as well as expressing appreciation to others throughout the day.

Daily Affirmations.
- ❖ I trust that all is well, and everything works for my highest good.
- ❖ I create clear and focused intentions to what I desire and allow the unfolding.
- ❖ Action is inspired by clarity and impulses.
- ❖ Co-create with fun, joy, pleasure and excitement!
- ❖ I visualize what I desire my day to be. I visualize the fun of my cruises. In visualizing I'm not attached to a particular outcome, sometimes the Universe has a better vision than I

do! Some mentors will say to end a vision with, "this or something better".

- ❖ Daily exercise and healthy eating habits are important to me in having a healthy body, mind and soul.
- ❖ My favorite affirmation is "I am Incredibly Blessed! Incredible Blessings flow to me with ease, in increasing amounts, from many different sources, on a continuous basis!"

One very important thing about stating affirmations and visualization is to really FEEL them! Work your way into actually being in that space of visualizing and feeling the joy, feeling the fun, feeling the satisfaction! Each of my mentors emphasizes feeling is so important: leaning into and living your desires. It feels amazing to be in alignment with your desires!

> *"Change your thoughts and you change your world."*
> ~ Norman Vincent Peale

The secret is to simply relax in the knowing that this strong desire within you knows when and how everything will work out for your highest good according to your desires. In relaxing and listening to your inner knowing (intuition) you will feel the nudges to take that next step which may be a baby step or a big step. One huge lesson for me has been noticing that the dream of living on a cruise ship and also the dream of getting my master's degree in social work

BECOMING THE MANIFESTING DIVA

were both dreams that I "decided" many years ago. This is what I want to do. I never once worried about how or when; I never put out any big effort or "worry" to make sure they happened. They were simply stated desires that I believed in. And both happened in their own timing with nudges of action along the way and turned out wonderfully! Manifesting your dreams will happen naturally as a result of your decisions and positive intentions.

About the Author

Karla Kopp, LMSW has had a 30+ year career working with people in crisis. She spent the first 15 years of her career as a social worker for Children's Services supporting children in foster care and their families. The second 15 years of her career, Karla worked in hospitals caring for patients and families in their plan of care towards a safe discharge. Working with people in crisis has made Karla passionate about improving her own health and life to Live, Laugh, Love, and Learn towards her Dream Come True. While on that journey of *Evolving on Purpose: Co-creating with the Divine*, she has a strong passion to educate and raise awareness that the time to take control of your life is NOW.

Karla has witnessed so much pain and despair that could have been avoided by being present, tuning into the Divine within, and working towards the life you would absolutely love – no matter what anyone else tells you and no matter what your current circumstances are.

Karla is more cognizant than ever in listening to her Divine within: her longings and her discontents that lead her to fulfilling her dreams. Karla's favorite mantra is: "I am Happy, Healthy, Wealthy, Joy-filled, FUN, and in love with life!"

Karla is currently retired and living her dream of living on cruise ships. She believes in creating a healthy mindset because your thoughts create your feelings which create your actions that create your results. She is excited to guide you in discovering a passion that lights you up and moves you towards your dreams come true.

Karla is a certified Life and Health Coach with The Health Coach Institute and The Brave Thinking Institute as well as a Certified Infinite Possibilities Trainer with Mike Dooley.

Connect with Karla below:

- Email: KarlaKopp@gmail.com

KATIE CAREY

Manifesting Your Magical Life

As a child, I was a daydreamer. Many children got in trouble for daydreaming at school, but not me. Even in a strict Catholic school, my teachers would allow me to release my creativity - of course, after I had finished my work. I realise now that I was a gifted child. I was brought up in a Catholic school from ages five to nine. I firmly believed in God and the angels, but not in the way it was discussed in school or church. Even then, I thought most of what they said was nonsense. Even then, I felt very different. I believed that God was not a man in the sky but something inside of me that I could always access. I did not need to be in a church to access my connection with God.

My father had taught me how to read and write before I started school. He was very ill and lost his job when I was five. My mum worked long hours at the local factory to make ends meet but didn't earn much there. I was learning all the songs I could learn because I had already decided the way out of our problems was for me to become an actress and a singer like Elvis Presley, The Osmonds, and every other famous superstar that I had watched on TV (in black and white until we got a colour TV on my 10th birthday).

Without knowing it, my focus was so powerful on my dreams, but now, with hindsight, I can see how I manifested them. I began singing in the school playground at age five and building audiences. A lovely dinner lady "Mrs Morgan" who was supervising us in the school playground at lunchtime, would give me a gift almost every time I sang, and everyone was happy, joyful, and clapping. I loved it.

My auntie got married when I was seven. I can't remember whether I was invited to sing or if I just stood up on that chair, belting out a rendition of *Paper Roses* when everyone began cheering, clapping, and giving me standing ovations.

When I was nine years old, I lost my first Nan, and she was the reason we were in Catholic school. So, promptly after she passed away, my dad took us out of that school, and we went to a Church of England school closer to home. He was not religious, but he had been in the British Army and married my Mum, an English Protestant, so he was becoming more and more resistant to us being in a Catholic school. He particularly hated that we were punished at school for not attending church every Sunday.

I loved our new school. I got to play my first speaking role in a school play all about the Coventry Blitz, but soon, I got caught up in a few physical fights in that school protecting my brother. My dad also taught me and my brother how to defend ourselves through boxing. Many years later, after my dad's passing, my brother became a professional boxer in his 30s and fought Amir Khan. Even though Amir beat him, my brother was the only opponent he could not take down and would not allow himself to be knocked out! I've often joked that I was my brother's first sparring partner.

There was, amidst the chaos and violence of our childhood, something that my dad also instilled in us: *"There's no such thing as can't."* We've both been pretty resilient because of this powerful core belief. Sadly, years later, my dad showed us that he couldn't stop drinking the alcohol that killed him at the tender age of 48. Once I moved up to secondary school, more opportunities opened up for me, which is somewhat unusual for an inner-city school. The theatre, music, and sports departments at Sidney Stringer School in the eighties were incredible.

My talents were noticed, and I was strongly encouraged to audition for the school shows, usually picking up a fantastic solo part until the really big one in 1982. I got the lead role playing the *"Little Match Girl."* (I will share more details about this in my solo books that are now being created.) One magical thing after another occurred for me, and by age fifteen, I found myself starring in a BBC TV series. While working on the series *"Anna of the Five Towns"*, I was offered the starring role in a BBC Radio 4 drama, *"Winnie Holden's Angel"*, playing the lead role of Winnie Holden. The TV Series and the Radio Drama aired the same week because I was debuting, playing my first role on TV and my first role on Radio the same week. It was so unusual for a new actor that I was also featured in the Sunday Times and the Radio Times that week.

My dreams were continually coming true, and I had my version of God and spirit. I felt that the spirit of my Nan was always with me at every step of that journey. My beliefs were solid. *"There is no such thing as can't."* I was on a lucky streak, it seemed, with magical experiences until I reached eighteen.

I was an adult, and my parents told me, "You need to get a real job to pay for board and lodgings."

My agent told me, "You need to get a real job and save to go to drama school." I had no money to travel to auditions up and down the country, but even when I did manage to find a way, I was met with rejection after rejection. I needed eight professional contracts to get my equity card, and I had submitted nine and was given a letter of exemption to take to auditions. On my next contract, I would receive my equity card, proof that I was an official Actors' Equity Association (AEA) member. An equity card was a tricky thing to get back then. I hadn't been to drama school but had worked nine professional contracts for acting and singing. When I showed the letter to the directors at every audition, I was met with a strange look - like they hadn't seen one of those before, so I was met with more rejection, and I gave up trying.

My luck had all dried up. I got a job in telesales selling textured wall coating by cold-calling people from telephone directories. I was only paid a basic salary plus commissions, and I hated it. I quickly moved on to another job while saving to attend drama school. I liked my new career as an operator at British Telecom. While working there, I met my first husband through a mutual friend. We dated for a couple of months before things began to get serious. He was in the Army, so I knew big changes would be coming for both of us.

Two years later, I lived 200 miles away in Salisbury and worked another horrible job. Eventually, I went back to British Telecom. While working there, I had my first psychic intuitive encounter on my way to work. On a one-hour bus journey, I suddenly went into a panic. I was having my first panic attack, but I had never heard of those before. By the time I got to work, I was crying inconsolably, saying, "My grandad is dying. I must go home." More of this story can be found in the chapter I wrote in *Intuitive: Knowing Her Truth*, the first book collaboration I participated in.

On arriving back in Coventry, I held my grandad's hand as he passed away. I was devastated. We had lost my husband's mum just before we married, so this was another traumatic event for us. I loved my grandparents dearly.

BECOMING THE MANIFESTING DIVA

Soon after this happened, I discovered that we were all about to be made redundant in my workplace, as they were closing our telephone exchange. As it happened, we were trying to have a baby and were posted to Northern Ireland, so receiving £5,000 in redundancy back in 1991 was a blessing to us, and retraining was an excellent package for me. I had only been there a year, and we were moving anyway—an excellent start for our new family. And because of this, I purchased my first-ever computer!

Three children manifested into my world every two years. I loved being a mum, but I didn't love the constant upheaval that military life brought. We moved house almost yearly, and twice we lived in Germany. Things didn't work out for that marriage, and we divorced after 17 years. Towards the end, I was diagnosed with depression and began taking antidepressants. Now, I know my intuition was trying to tell me something, but I was ignoring her. Eventually, I listened, began looking for the evidence, and discovered enough to show me that it was time to walk away.

I went on to manifest exactly what I didn't want next: an alcohol-dependent second husband. You can read more about that in my chapter in *Entangled No More,* but what I want to share with you in this chapter is what happened once that cycle of manifesting trauma after trauma in my life ended in 2020.

I had reached the tender age of 52, having manifested a toxic marriage, another awful job, and disabling health conditions. I finally got thirteen years into the marriage, divorced for a second time, and changed my name back to Katie Carey. It was as if the girl I used to be had reappeared, the daydreaming child who believed anything was possible. I had just come through over a decade of learning all about the Law of Attraction, manifestation, and universal laws. After I changed my name, I was tapping into a new identity: the playful, dreamlike, curious version of me that I once was as a child and teenager.

First, I launched the Soulfulvalley Podcast, and it charted at launch. I watched in amazement as my podcast began to go up into the global rankings. I was in a coaching group called the LightWeb, which was sheer magic. Amazing things began to happen for me. Large sums of money manifested to support me as I was on my journey of loving myself and starting to build my online business.

Through the coaching, I connected with many magical humans worldwide and interviewed some of them. I felt as joyful as I was when I was acting and singing in my teens, and then my dream of becoming a best-selling author landed in my lap. Days after I set the intention to call that in, I found myself invited to the opportunity by a stranger named *Brigid Holder* in my direct messages on Facebook Messenger. Shortly after, we launched that book, I created my own publishing house, and one after the other, the books I launched became number 1 on Amazon's best-seller lists in multiple countries. I was in my element. I have loved books since I was a toddler, and I'm addicted to them in physical form and on the Kindle. I'm always reading, and now I'm creating them, too!

The universe would send in support at each stage when business felt difficult. *Katische Haberfield* (who went on to co-author

BECOMING THE MANIFESTING DIVA

Entangled No More) invited me to appear on her podcast, *The Infinite Life* and offered to deliver past life regression sessions to me, asking if they could go live on her podcast. At first, I was scared. I've sat in mediumship circles, been on psychic development courses, and always avoided past life regressions, but now, my intuition told me it was time.

Katische's sessions immediately unlocked my past wounds regarding money and relationships. After the podcast, the income in my business improved, and my current boyfriend arrived. Our first date was synchronistically aligned with the release of our podcast episode. Everything unfolded in a uniquely magical way. More of that story is in *Evolving on Purpose: Co-creating with the Divine.*

Over the last couple of years, I've received many lessons and teachings. We've manifested a new home together. My boyfriend manifested the perfect job practically on our doorstep! I manifested the sale of my house… twice. I trained in the Akashic Records last year and discovered how much magic is available to us when we open our hearts and minds, are decisive about what we want, and must ask our spirit team to help us.

The biggest shock was when I manifested the opportunity to be featured in the movie/documentary *Zero Limits,* which *Dr. Joe Vitale* created. This occurred following another session with *Katische*. I spotted the synchronicity following my session with her - a post with an opportunity to apply for the movie, which I promptly recognised and jumped on. I came away from my interview with the thought that if I were supposed to be in a movie called *"Zero Limits"*, there would be no limits to me being a part of that. One synchronicity after another occurred, and I am excited to share that a few weeks ago, I was filmed for my feature in the documentary. I still can't quite believe I did that, and you will now see that *Dr. Joe Vitale* wrote this book foreword! When I announced this to my authors, one of them told me that she had manifested this because she thought, *wouldn't it be great if Dr. Joe Vitale wrote our book foreword?* She had not said this to me at any point, but clearly, we were all on the same wavelength. After all, learning about manifesting began with Dr. Joe over a decade ago for me.

    Life can be fun when you focus on loving yourself, closing the door to toxic relationships, and raising your standards and boundaries. When we stay stuck in our disempowered victim stories—feeling that everything is happening to us and out of our control—that's precisely what we experience. But when we shift into "everything is happening for me," life unfolds magically. In my experience, we get what we believe in and decide what we deserve.

    Just a couple of weeks ago, I had been into the Akashic Records and asked my guides to remove anything in the way of my house selling for myself and the person out there who would love to buy it. I trusted that this would help to shift things in the right direction. After the first person buying had pulled out, it had been a long time coming. The following day, I told my boyfriend what I had done in the Akashic records, and I declared out loud, "*Simpson West* is going to call me today with an offer, and I will accept." Later that day, when the phone rang with my estate agent's name, we both had stunned faces because that's precisely what happened.

I left my chapter until almost the last in the book was written because I knew the book was waiting for some more magic to occur. Manifesting literally can happen based on the strength of the conviction of your words. I have so many examples that I will be writing a whole book on these topics soon. In the meantime, focus on building self-trust, self-belief, and self-worth. Remember that your spirit team is just waiting to support you in the wings of this stage called life, and you get to play the lead role. As your story magically unfolds, you will experience the magic and find the miracles in the simplest everyday things.

I look forward to sharing more magic and miracles with you in the next chapter and my next solo book.

I bid you all Happy Magical Manifesting.

About the Author

Katie Carey, an International Best-Selling Author, is the CEO of Katie Carey Media LTD and the founder of Soulful Valley Publishing House. She is also the host of the Soulful Valley podcast, a globally ranked podcast in the Top 1%. Through her podcast and multi-author books, Katie provides a platform for spiritual entrepreneurs, visionary artists, coaches, energy healers, authors, and conscious creators to elevate their visibility. Previously, Katie founded STAGES, an alternative mental health charity, and strongly advocates for mental health, disability, and emotional well-being. Having experienced mobility issues that led to her early retirement at the age of 48, Katie is particularly passionate about supporting individuals in these areas, drawing from her journey.

With a love for blending science and spirituality, Katie collaborates with like-minded individuals in her multi-author books. Many authors have shared stories of synchronicities that led to their collaboration with Katie. She aims to bring these concepts and ideas

BECOMING THE MANIFESTING DIVA

to a broader audience, supporting mental, spiritual, emotional, and physical well-being.

Katie's background includes work in TV, Radio, and Theatre as an actress and singer, which she pursued from a young age. She is transitioning from living in Northamptonshire, where she has lived for 22 years, to moving to Oakham, Rutland, in the UK and is a proud Mum to three adult children and a loving grandmother. Katie is dedicated to educating and empowering people to find healthier solutions and break free from ancestral, toxic, and generational patterns of lack and trauma. She actively raises consciousness through her roles as a mentor, coach, podcaster, author, and publisher and through her songs and poetry.

If you want to collaborate with Katie on one of her multi-author books, be a guest on her podcast, write your solo book, or learn more about her one-on-one coaching, healing, or mentorship services.

Connect with Katie below:

- https://pensight.com/x/soulfulvalley
- https://apple.co/3BkJdkn

KATIE GAUTHIER

Crossroads to Opportunities

I am the Queen of Manifesting Opportunities.

When I find myself needing money, the opportunity to work overtime, an unexpected job offer, or even a sudden windfall will appear seemingly out of nowhere. But how? That's the beauty of the universe and co-creating with it. The universe knows your limits and will not push more than that onto you at any given time. The universe matches energy better than anyone, and it's our job to align ourselves with our highest good and seek out the opportunities that the universe throws our way.

BECOMING THE MANIFESTING DIVA

Another way that the universe will present opportunities to us is through "crossroads moments." A crossroad moment is when you have two choices that will inevitably have a huge impact on the rest of your life. My best example of this would be when I was deep in the throes of mental illness. At my absolute lowest, I was presented with a crossroads moment that brought me to the only possible outcome: life as I knew it needed to end.

My choices were to either give in to the intrusive thoughts and allow everything to go dark one last time or I could seek help and start the climb out of that deep, dark hole that was my mind. As you're currently reading this, it's safe to assume that I chose to end that life in the best possible way: by building a new one altogether.

It took a sprained foot to get me to drive myself to the hospital in the first place, and I have never been more grateful for an injury. While filling out the intake form at the emergency department, I was again met with a crossroads moment: do I write down that I think I broke my foot and leave it at that? Or do I include the suicidal ideation? As terrifying as it was, I made a point of writing down "I think I broke my foot, and I am suicidal" on that intake form and awaited my turn to be called upon by the triage nurse. From there, things become a bit blurry. They sent me for a series of X-rays and put me in a secure room pretty quickly so that I would have some privacy.

I remember speaking with several staff members, including nursing staff, a social worker, and several doctors. They determined that I was not an immediate threat to myself or others as I had maintained composure throughout the intake process, and they gave me another crossroads moment. Still, one thing was certain: I was not going home that day.

The last crossroads moment I was given that day was to either stay put at the local hospital, or I could be transferred to a psychiatric hospital in the nearest city, roughly two hours away by ambulance. I remember the doctor clarifying that the facility in the city would remain an option should my condition worsen beyond the capabilities of the local hospital, so I opted to stay put. To say that I was terrified is a gross understatement, but it is the only word that seems to express my feelings at the time. My whole body felt numb. Every step felt like I was wearing lead shoes. Everything felt so surreal, as if I was moving in slow motion. I remember the nurses were so kind and caring towards me, making sure that I was as comfortable as one can be in a hospital bed before leaving me for the night.

The following two weeks were an absolute blur of therapies, medication trials, and even more therapy. I connected with a few other patients, and it helped to know that I was not the only one struggling with the recovery process. Knowing that others had had similar experiences and came out the other side solidified that I would have to put in the work if I wanted to get better.

And that's exactly what I did.

Fast forward a few years, and I can honestly say that my life has been 100% co-created with the universe. I decided that I needed a change in a big way. The universe brought an opportunity to move across the country. I needed a better-paying job, and the company I worked for was hiring for a better-paying position. I did not get that job, but that was a great thing because that rejection prompted me to look outside the box.

Today, I am making more money than ever before, working for a great company and for myself. Even the opportunity to write this chapter in this book was manifested. This feels as if it was destined to happen.

If you find yourself struggling with manifesting, try not to think about it as the universe handing things to you on a silver platter. That's not how that works. The universe is much more subtle than that at first. It will offer up opportunities that you can choose to either accept with open arms or disregard altogether, leaving you on the same path until it's time to circle back and learn a new lesson. Which, again, you can choose to either accept or disregard. That's what's so beautiful about co-creating with the universe: the choice is ultimately yours. You can keep spinning your wheels hoping for progress, or you can keep moving forward, looking for opportunities and nods from the universe as you go. I promise you, moving forward has always worked better for me than staying put when it comes to improving my life and actually enjoying it for what it is and what it isn't. Thinking about it now, it makes one of my tattoos – literally saying, "Keep moving forward" – all the more appropriate.

I'm forever grateful for my crossroads moments, especially the most pivotal one that changed the entire course of my life. One decision is all it takes to change your whole life. You must decide and follow through by taking the appropriate steps. Yes, it's a challenge. But more importantly, it is so, so very worth it. So now, dear reader, I ask: what will you choose the next time the universe offers up an opportunity for growth? Will you take action? Or will you stay stagnant? The choice is yours.

Remember that taking action does not need to be huge leaps and bounds. Start small. Aim to improve by a mere 1% daily, and after a relatively short amount of time, you will see significant progress. This is not only based on research but also on personal experience.

When I was obese, I decided that I would compete in the bikini division of a bodybuilding show. In order to hit this goal, I hired a coach who was less than optimistic about my outcome, but nevertheless, we moved on with the plan for me to compete. In under six months, I not only managed to lose a significant amount of weight (over 70 lbs), but on show day, I placed 7th and won the *Most Inspirational Journey Award* for the entire show. It was an incredible and humbling experience. A few months later, I decided to compete again in a different city, and that time, I placed 6th in my category, which goes to show that when someone tells you that you can't do something, you should do it twice – and take pictures! The naysayers will always be around to doubt you and your conviction to attain your goals. Use them as fuel because the doubters and their comments do not matter at the end of the day.

You are much more powerful and capable than you realize. During my formative years, I dealt with extreme stress levels and copious amounts of trauma rather than having a typical adolescence. The way I see it, if someone like me can learn the skills required to move forward, anyone can. We can learn to take life by the hand and say "It's okay, we're safe now. Let's find a new path."

If you're reading this and thinking to yourself, "Katie, how could you possibly know what I've been through?! Do you know my trauma? Do you know my stress?" Well, no. I don't. This is something that I will admit – your story, your trauma, and your stress are as unique as you are.

This isn't a chapter to tell you what to do. This is a chapter to give hope. This demonstrates that people can come back from even the worst-case scenarios. I wish that you find peace. I pray that you find inspiration in my journey and decide for yourself that you are worth investing in, improving and loving. You are worth it. Full stop.

Before closing out this chapter, I would like to lead you through one of my favorite mindfulness exercises that has helped me tremendously over the years, and I hope it has a similar effect on you.

First, we'll start by taking a deep breath through the nose (ideally for a 5-7 second count). Then, slowly exhale for a 7-10 count through the mouth. Repeat this several times if you must, focusing on your breath and the different sensations. Perhaps the air feels cool as it enters your nostrils, and slightly warmer as it leaves through your mouth.

Now, we're going to change gears. Continue breathing in through the nose and out through the mouth, and I'd like you to take notice of five things you can *see*. Any five things will do.

Have you made a mental note of these five things?

Good.

Well done.

Now, I'd like you to listen—really listen to your surroundings. This time, we'll make a mental note of four things that we can hear. These can be any environmental sounds: your breath, cars driving by outside, birds chirping, music playing, and so on.

Have you noticed four sounds?

Perfect!

Next, we are going to hone in on our sense of *touch*. What are three things that you are currently *feeling*? This one can be a bit trickier, so take your time to notice the sensations against your skin.

Once you've made that mental note, we're going to come to our olfactory senses and take a sniff at the air. At this time, I'd like to invite you to take note of two things that you can *smell*.

Finally, we are coming to our final sense for this exercise. What is one thing that you can *taste*? Perhaps the remnants of your last sip of coffee or tea?

Now that we've managed to activate our parasympathetic nervous system with that breathing technique and come back to the present moment with our 5, 4, 3, 2, 1 senses countdown, I hope that you are feeling a sense of relief and grounding wash over you.

BECOMING THE MANIFESTING DIVA

I wanted to share this exercise because it not only affords us the opportunity to notice our surroundings but also helps to bring us back into our immediate surroundings. This is how simple mindfulness can be. This is how we can reconnect with ourselves and become more open to the signs and offerings given to us by the universe.

In closing, I want to take the opportunity to remind you that you are capable, worthy, and loved. I hope you've enjoyed this chapter and have found it useful in some way. Now, dear reader, I hope you realize just how magnificent you are – exactly as you are – in this very moment. I hope you can take the reins and co-create with the universe in your own way. Go build your dream life.

You deserve it.

About the Author

Katie Gauthier is a mom of two incredible teenagers and likes to refer to herself as a "Kate of All Trades," because she collects certifications like Pokémon cards and has a variety of interests that she pursues regularly. To date, she is a certified belief-clearing practitioner, Hatha yoga teacher, Yin yoga teacher, spiritual coach, black belt in HapKiDo, author, trauma survivor, mental health advocate, bikini competitor, meditation teacher, and entrepreneur. She is also working towards her Yoga Therapist certification.

Katie specializes in setting audacious goals and accelerating the process of attaining them by using all her acquired skills. Her primary goal in life is to live it fully and help others heal from the things they don't necessarily talk about to get them on track to living their best lives.

Katie unapologetically uses her unique perspective, and keen sense of humor to help clients – and all in her energetic field – feel at ease and welcome exactly as they are. She is certain that life can always be better when we choose to live authentically based on her

BECOMING THE MANIFESTING DIVA

personal experiences. Her business is called "Elevate Yoga and Wellness" because Katie believes in the power of moving up to the next level by connecting and balancing mind, body, and spirit.

In Katie's experience, connecting and balancing mind, body, and spirit allows for a much easier means of releasing trauma and all that no longer serves the individual. This release creates space for new habits that align with the individual's idea of their dream life. Katie likes to use herself as a primary example of how one can go from rock bottom to living an incredible life with the right strategies and practices.

Connect with Katie below:

- https://www.elevateyogawellness.ca
- https://www.amazon.ca/stores/author/B0DDR1TFM4
- https://linktr.ee/katiegee

LOUISE SAMOSORN

If You Believe, Then You Will Receive

I've always been a dreamer, an optimist, an everything-is-going-to-be-okay kind of girl. As a kid, I spent many afternoons lying on the grass, soaking up the warmth of the sun. I would stare up at the sky and the big fluffy clouds and create figures and characters out of them. I spent countless hours climbing in the trees, swinging from branch to branch while pretending to live in a fantasy world far from reality.

By the time I had reached my teen years, society had sunk its claws in, and the dreamer in me started to fade. The clouds didn't seem so fascinating anymore. I didn't feel safe. I didn't feel heard, so I found comfort in drugs, alcohol and being a delinquent. I didn't have anyone to look up to. Everyone around me was just getting by, so I felt doomed to a life of mediocrity and gave up trying. I decided at that point that success just wasn't written in the stars for me.

I didn't do any inner work, and the uncertainty and chaos showed up in my life on the outside. I found myself in dead-end job after dead-end and one toxic relationship after another. I was a self-destructing, ticking time bomb ready to explode at any time. Substance abuse and a poor mentality controlled my thoughts, emotions, and motives. Something had to change.

At age 25, I thought that changing my environment was the answer, so I did something drastic and bought a one-way plane ticket from Australia to the UK. Although it became a time of fond memories and friendships, I still felt a deep sense of loneliness and sadness, so much so that I couldn't remember the last time I had actually heard myself laugh.

I discovered that I had a passion for travelling and experiencing new cultures, new food, and new friends. This sent me on an extended expedition throughout southeast Asia, where I spent two years travelling and working. I tried to keep the demons at bay, but often, my old habits would always come knocking, and it just became a vicious cycle. No matter where I was in the world. On the outside, I seemed like a well-travelled, culture-seeking, confident nomad, but inside, I was still a lost little 14-year-old, Just trying to find her way in the world.

On the morning of Monday, 15th April 2013, I received the call no one wants to receive, especially when you are 7800 kilometres from home. My brother had passed away in his sleep at age 38. His body decided it was time to rest after decades of heavy substance abuse, and his soul was finally set free from his demons.

Only hours before this devastating call, I had what I can only describe as one of the most peaceful, fulfilling mornings I had ever had. I was living in Luang Prabang, a beautiful, quaint, and deeply spiritual town in the north of Laos. It was Laos New Year, a week-long festivity of water fights and festivals.

For whatever reason, I just didn't feel like partying the night before, which I did almost every night, but instead, I just wanted to be home in peace. Although I tossed and turned all night, I woke up just as the sun rose, and I remember feeling so light and content in that moment. I did something I had never done while living there: I walked down to local morning markets and bought fresh produce to make the biggest bacon and egg fry up (something I hadn't eaten in a while). The whole process, from cooking to sitting on the front deck in the morning sunshine, listening to the morning birds and roosters, was such a peaceful and beautiful moment. A reminder I know my brother sent me to slow down, appreciate, and be grateful for all the beauty and simple things in life. That morning changed me in ways that would go on to shape the next decade of my life.

Stepping into my 30s was really like stepping into a whole new chapter. I started choosing myself, and I started choosing life to see the beauty and the blessings right in front of me. My brother's passing really shook me to my core for many reasons, but the most

BECOMING THE MANIFESTING DIVA

significant catalyst for me was that he died at age 38, having achieved very little with no desire or direction.

I genuinely felt sorry for him that he never got to experience life on a deeper level with all its joy and beauty. At this point, I knew I had to change for things to change. I began to see life differently. I began to see the opportunities I had available – the power within myself to quantum leap and create a life I felt proud to star in. But first, I had to know what that looked like before I could create it.

I dove deep into self-reflection, mindset, and personal development through either books, online courses, or mentoring, which fast-tracked my personal growth. In the space of 8 years, I married the love of my life – the yin to my yang – a man who makes me feel safe and loved unconditionally. I birthed three amazing, perfect humans, established and operated three businesses that grew from nothing to multi-six figures, found spirituality, and manifested a beautiful home to raise my family surrounded by nature, overlooking the largest lake in the southern hemisphere. Only eight years prior, I was working a dead-end job, lost emotionally and mentally with no direction. How did I turn everything around so fast?

First, I had to get really honest with myself and understand my unique passion and purpose. This required deep soul searching and dreaming big – so big to the point that it scared me. Once I had my vision clear, I knew there was more to manifesting than just visualising my desires. The secret sauce is to put your desires out into the universe, surrender to the how, and then take aligned action every day to do my part in co-creating. The last part is the step that most people miss. They release their dreams to the universe, surrender, sit on their hands and wait. Then, they wonder why their dreams aren't becoming their reality.

We are always co-creating with Source, God, the universe with every action we take – both good and bad. Be specific each time you share with the universe (out loud, of course) the desired outcome you wish to manifest into existence. A prime example: in December 2022, I attended a 3-day self-development retreat in a beautiful penthouse in Melbourne, Australia. Day 3 was a 'goals and vision day', and we could participate in making a vision board. I'll be honest: I'm not crazy about vision boards, so I wasn't invested and put things on there that would be nice to have or do, but nothing that set me on fire.

Fast-forward to February 2024. After returning from a healing retreat in Bali, the downloads from Source were coming in thick and fast, and this is where my women's self-love and wellness retreat was born. The idea just felt so right, something I was deeply passionate about. I quickly dove in and started to find the perfect villa in Phuket, Thailand. Then, it was time to put together the website and marketing.

Now, this is where creating the retreat gets wild. As I was selecting the images I wanted to use, I let out a squeal. The image on the screen was so familiar I couldn't believe it. I ran downstairs and retrieved the vision board from a year and a half prior, and there on my computer screen was almost image for image of what was right in the centre of the vision board. Upon closer inspection, I found that almost every image on the canvas was related to the retreat I was called to create. So, I had put it out into the universe that this was something I wanted to exist in my reality – which worked! The images on the canvas had manifested, but how they manifested wasn't precisely how I originally envisioned it. I missed that vital step. I wasn't specific or descriptive enough with my intention when I put the images out into the universe. However, I firmly believe that the vision board played out how the images were always meant to play out and that they came to life just on time.

Everyone has the ability to manifest. Manifestation is about being intentional with your actions. The best way to begin manifesting magic is to start with gratitude. You can share ten things you are grateful for every morning before getting out of bed or journal in the evening before bed about all the experiences you are grateful for that day. Daily gratitude is such a great way to lift your vibration. Another great way is to write down an affirmation of a desired outcome and repeat the affirmation three times daily, thanking the universe as though you have already received what you are asking for. Taking daily action is also required to co-create because manifesting is about creating the feeling, and the quickest way to create the feeling is by taking action.

I have spent almost a decade working on myself, quantum leaping, and creating a life I'm proud to have – a life that fulfils me with love and passion every day, with direction and intention. I am called to serve women, but it is more than a calling. I started listening to my intuition and following my heart; those actions in faith led me to my purpose.

I have invested almost two years coaching women as they seek to discover their own purpose. Often, these women have lost their identity after becoming mothers or being stuck in a long-term career that no longer excites them.

I guide them in discovering their passions, desires, and values. Together, we create sustainable daily actions so they too, can start manifesting a life full of joy and fulfilment. I predominantly coach one-on-one because having a coach in your back pocket keeping you accountable is the fastest way to quantum leap into the next and best version of you.

About the Author

Louise Samosorn is a dedicated wife and mother of three, a devoted spiritualist, and a personal growth and mindset coach. She is also an intuitive energy healer, speaker, and global self-love and wellness retreat facilitator. Women seek her mentorship and programs so they can rediscover their purpose and live a life of joy and fulfilment.

Louise's spiritual journey, unbeknownst to her at the time, actually began at a young age. After a constant struggle with mental illness and trying to find her place in this world, the death of her brother just over a decade ago sparked a journey of deep self-reflection, personal growth, and discovery. For the first time, she was able to understand her gifts and her soul's connection with the universe.

She believes our souls are sent to this earth for a reason, and she has dedicated her life to fulfilling that mission through having a coaching business that inspires women to align with their purpose.

Connect with Louise below:

- https://www.facebook.com/Louise.Samosorn.Coaching

MARIE SCHLEMM

Chocolate, Football, and the Tao

"We are all born mad. Some remain so."
~ Samuel Beckett

E*ierlegende Wollmilchsau* was the title of my job application.

It translates as "egg-laying wool milk sow. Someone who can do anything that is thrown at her. That's who they seemed to want. I had applied for a job at university to bolster my income. They didn't take me. It was the 90s. I guess they were not ready for me.

Have I changed since then? Have I become an "adult"?

BECOMING THE MANIFESTING DIVA

Now, I am a veterinary surgeon, a mother, a wife, and an ex-wife. I have dabbled with energy healing, breathwork, and making chocolate. I am also a vanlifer, a budding cocoa farmer, a grassroots activist in a small Ghanaian community, a FIFA licenced football (soccer) agent, a professional Football Scout, the owner of a successful Okada business in Tepa Ghana (Tuk Tuk in other countries), an aspiring millionairess, a world traveller, an online business owner, an explorer, an adventurer, a sea swimmer, a Kilimanjaro hiker, a lover of Salsa dancing and good food, and an occasional foul mouth.

Mr. Beckett did have a point. 2023 has been one of the most tumultuous, painful, yet amazing years of my life.

Have I manifested all this? Absolutely. Consciously and unconsciously, all of it intentionally. Even the negative.

"He said he'd be here this morning. It's 11:50!" I exclaimed, turning to David, my "partner in crime". He had traveled all the way to Ghana with me, to a small cocoa farming community out in the sticks.

David shrugged in response, fully embodying calmness and patience. He knew things were different and that it took longer in Africa since he had been there plenty of times. It was my first time, and I was glad I had him there!

I was getting impatient... *"Hummeln unter'm Hintern"* (German for "bumble bees under my bum"). I wanted to get stuff done.

Nelson had a lot on his plate. He was not just a cocoa farmer; he was also an assembly member, the equivalent of the mayor of his community. Everybody came to him with their issues. I understood, but still! When I was in the UK, we always communicated well. We could chat for hours on Messenger.

But all that would change as soon as we hit the ground in Ghana. There was no real communication. David and I were only given the necessary information about things we would do and when. Nelson said he grew up in child labour himself (which may or may not have happened). I gave him the benefit of the doubt.

"Perhaps he hasn't learned certain social and emotional skills."

The cultural differences became clearer, and wow! German and Ghanaian culture could almost not be more different!

Those were all the excuses and explanations I created, so I carried on despite some warning signs. Why on earth did I do all this? Why did I insist on going with the flow even when my gut told me to stop? Since the death of my son in 2004, I have become good at going with the flow. But I was not always great at listening to my intuition and "flowed" into not so nice experiences, then I adjusted and turned them into better experiences. That's why I called my company the "Tao of Chocolate": going with the flow, being present and aware. Chocolate taught me.

Two years before that scene in Ghana, during lockdown, I had started my online business. I wanted to create a different income than that of my vet job. So, I noticed some Facebook ads, responded to them, and found the necessary money to enrol in "how to do online marketing" courses, even in a high ticket coaching community. I loved it!

At the start of this learning journey I thought, "One day, I will find a cause to support." Approximately two weeks after that thought, the cause had found me. Talk about manifestation!

I first met Nelson during an online chocolate festival in October 2020. Then, I wanted to connect him with someone else from the online marketing community who wanted to know how he could make money with cocoa and chocolate. The connection between those 2 guys never happened, but Nelson and I started chatting. Tentative at first, several contacts from the sustainable cocoa movement in England confirmed that he is a real guy and that they like his work, so I carried on chatting, and we built up a really good connection… or so I thought.

I learned so much about life in Ghana, his past, his duties as an assembly member, and his cocoa farming.

"I want to make my own chocolate," he declared.

"Why? It's so hot in Ghana!" I exclaimed.

"Yes, it is hot, but making chocolate is the only way I can increase my income from the cacao, because I am not allowed to sell my beans privately."

Ghana is one of very few countries where the whole cocoa industry and trade is controlled by the government. The farmers receive approximately 50% of the price for the beans. The rest goes to the government. Atrocious. But, if Nelson starts processing the beans himself, then he can sell the products privately.

Once he had explained that, of course, I was in!

To get started as a chocolate maker, you only need three things:

1. Cacao beans (which Nelson had plenty on his farm)
2. A way to roast the beans (Nelson had an open fire), and
3. A small grinder

That grinder plus shipping cost about $400 to 500 USD. While the grinder did not cost a lot of money, I did not want to finance it all on my own, so I started fundraising.

With a bit of financial help, Nelson had his grinder in April 2021. Manifested in no time. I taught him how to make chocolate, and he got started, spreading chocolate joy in the community. Our connection got stronger; he felt like a brother from a different mother.

The next hurdle was thrown at us in April 2022. Nelson co-owned his farm, and the co-owners wanted to sell. In Ghana, when one of the co-owners wants to sell their portion of a property, they determine which part is being sold.

Since not all of the farm was cultivated, they wanted to sell the cultivated part to make the most profit. But then Nelson would have had to start from scratch! It takes about four years for a cocoa tree to bear fruit. His only other alternative was to give up and move to the city, which is what his wife wanted, but he didn't.

BECOMING THE MANIFESTING DIVA

"Do you trust me?" I asked him.

"Yes."

We needed at least $2,500 USD, and this was my plan: start a sponsorship for the cocoa trees!

The cause was amazing and beautiful because his income could enable him to work further in the communities, educate farmers, and help children attend school rather than work on the farm. He discussed it with his wife and said, "Ok, let's do it!"

I created a beautiful campaign and manifested almost $4,000 USD within five days.

Boom!

This was one of the very conscious manifestations.

I know that when I am 100% behind something and convinced of its goodness (as I was at the time) when I don't have any doubts, I can achieve it.

The first time I realised I had done this was when I was still married with two little girls, and we moved house, location, school, and work in 2000. We lived south of Wimbledon, London. We had looked at a Steiner (Waldorf) school a good hour away in a small village. We both wanted our children to go there, but it seemed out of reach. The school was too expensive, the move would be too stressful, and finding new jobs would be too challenging.

We looked again and decided, "This is it! We are changing schools and everything that comes with it!" My husband was willing to drive a long distance to work at the time, so I started looking for a new job. A little while later, on the same day and almost at the same time, we got the approval from school and the approval from my new job! Amazing.

We had four wonderful and tumultuous years there. Not all of it was smooth sailing; I had a lot of ups and deep downs. My ex and I were not always present for our daughters, and then I got pregnant again. He didn't want any more children. I could not even think about termination. In the end, he came around, and we were looking forward to number three.

After the full nine months, in February 2004, came the start of my and our biggest transformation. I started going into labour, but after a few hours, everything stopped, and we were sent to the hospital.

Our baby had died.

We were sent home with empty hands and a broken heart.

Shock turned into turmoil, which then turned into hysteria: "I NEED a caesarian section NOW!" I screamed to my doctor over the phone.

"This is not an emergency. We can't do a c-section. You need to wait."

"NO! This is a *psychological* emergency!"

Eventually, I gave up. I asked Amanda, my acupuncturist and pregnancy yoga teacher, to come for some acupuncture the next day. She helped me surrender. I was scheduled to deliver my dead baby the next day. Another friend came for support, and she was an absolute gift from heaven.

I surrendered.

BECOMING THE MANIFESTING DIVA

"It's your labour and your baby's birth." Amanda had always said that in our yoga sessions, but now it all made sense. Now, it was time for MY labour.

It was my most beautiful and most painful labour, a quite surreal experience. We cried, we laughed, we cried again. I screamed my loudest and most painful screams when he was born. It was the first step of my grieving and letting go process.

He was born with very big feet compared to my daughters.

He had to carry us – carry *me* – a long way.

Dark days and weeks followed until I finally was ready to do something about it.

My therapy was working with chocolate.

Chocolate requires presence, patience, and surrender.

From being a very impatient student, asking, "Do I really have to do this tempering thing?! Ugh!" I turned into a great student and a great chocolatier whose chocolates sold. They were different. Fresh, rich, luxurious, and has a short shelf life due to the lack of glucose syrups, sorbitol, and other toxic ingredients. The lack of all that, plus the use of the best chocolate from Venezuela, ensured an amazing taste. I had fans.

Unfortunately, my business sense wasn't as good—not at all. I went back to veterinary work and gave up chocolate-making as a business.

A few years later, I separated from my husband, severely damaged my relationship with my daughters in the process, got divorced, dabbled with different energy healing modalities, trained as a breath worker, qualified as a Galen Myotherapist, developed an increasing awareness of all the evil that was really going on in the cocoa industry (child labour, slavery, and child trafficking galore – ALL common supermarket brands know and tolerate it), then COVID caused lockdowns in 2020, and I found my connection with a small cocoa farming community in Ghana.

So, I had manifested the money Nelson needed for his farm through fundraising and my own finances, and he could buy it outright. We were feeling on top of the world! Then, I wanted to help him increase the quality of his beans so that he and I could make a first-class tree-to-bar chocolate together.

That was the reason for my first trip to Ghana. I needed an expert, and David Greenwood-Haigh, an international chocolate consultant, donated his time and wisdom to accompany me. I paid for his flights and our accommodation, and off we went.

We spent three weeks in Ghana in October 2022. It was wonderful.

We introduced the sponsors to their trees, helped with harvesting, experimented with a different fermentation method, roasted, winnowed, and ground the beans, made chocolate, cocoa vinegar, cocoa juice, husk tea, cocoa nib "coffee", visited the cocoa research institute near Accra, and woke up at the crack of dawn to see all the pollinators on the farm.

Nelson's farm is absolutely beautiful. He has been farming organically for the last 2-3 years and managed the farm as an agroforestry farm. I loved it. On one part of his farm that didn't have any cocoa trees yet, we were thinking of building some platforms that could be used for retreats. They would be on a slope with the most amazing views over the jungle.

Nelson also introduced me to the community's football team, Heaven Stars, and to one particular young man: officially, A.T. Dominic Twum. A.T. was tall, dark, and handsome, a bit shy, and very polite. He was a warm and big-hearted, welcoming, and very sympathetic young man who had already experienced more trauma in his 18 years than any person should have in an entire lifetime.

"We have a lot of talent out here, but they won't be spotted. No scout comes out this far," Nelson told me. "But our talent here is better than what is now in the premier league teams. Unfortunately, only rich kids get to play professionally."

"I have no idea about football," I remarked, "but I am good at connecting people. We need some videos, and once I'm back in the UK, I'll start talking."

And talk I did. David sent me a link to a free webinar about becoming a football agent, which I didn't even know existed.

I also started chatting to A.T. because he kept hiding behind Nelson, getting him to translate any football-related stuff.

"Oh no, no, no!" I said. "If you ever want to go to Europe, you had better improve your English." We met regularly for WhatsApp video calls, and his English improved quickly while we got to know each other.

He is one of the good ones. A good kid. Although, I can't really call him a kid. He is a fully grown and very tall young man who, in many ways, is mature far beyond his years. His mom died in his lap on the way to the hospital when he was eight years old. He lived in extreme poverty and constantly had to worry about his own survival and his sister's. He was fortunate enough to have fatherly guidance from Richard, one of the village's pastors and the Heaven Stars manager.

While I discovered all this about A.T., I also learned more about becoming a football agent, and I actually became one. In April 2023, I sat the first FIFA exam for Football Agents in Accra, Ghana (since I was in Ghana at that time anyway), and I passed it!

Hope.

He finally had hope—and not just any hope—realistic hope—hope that his dreams now actually have a chance to turn into reality. That is what changed for A.T. and all the other players from Heaven Stars and the ones who will come after them when I started involving myself with football.

I gave them hope.

There is no work in the Ghanaian community. If you're lucky, you own farmland where you can earn a pitiful amount with cocoa farming or grow plant foods for your own family.

Other than that, there is very little.

The young footballers have a community: their football club. They don't need drugs or alcohol or crime. The club is their second family, and membership in the club comes with an ethos and stability that some of them don't have at home. It's a beautiful group of caring young men. We need more of those – especially in football.

BECOMING THE MANIFESTING DIVA

Unfortunately, Nelson grew upset and jealous that I devoted more time to football. He was concerned about my ability to run two separate projects simultaneously: football and chocolate. I can easily run two projects at the same time—especially if they are two projects that I am passionate about and that go beautifully hand in hand—but not everybody can see that.

He stopped talking to me, broke off our relationship without any particular reason, and we went our separate ways.

The feelings that come up are my internal confirmation that I am on the right path: I feel excited, full of energy, and passionate.

My external confirmation is how big my network is and how fast it is growing. My veterinary network is small. When I started my Tao of Chocolate online, the chocolate network grew bigger and faster than the veterinarian ever has. And now, the football network?! Oh my. It's outgrown both of them.

The separation from Nelson hit me hard. He really felt like a brother from another mother. I could see our differences more clearly in April 2023 during my last visit. We had some arguments, and I made big mistakes as well. There was no talking about it, though, and there was no openness to forgive.

Nevertheless, my purpose and passion remain—educating the world about and changing the dark reality of the cocoa industry, and, also, with the help of football, changing children's lives.

I am picking up my pieces, putting myself back together, and carrying on. I have other partners in Ghana, and there are many more communities that I would love to get to know in Ghana and beyond.

One of the most important things I have learned is that we have to be more open than we thought we could be. We have to be open to forgiveness. We need to forgive the misunderstandings we create due to our cultural differences. For example, I ask questions to understand something. If I ask questions in Ghana, it is often an insult because I inadvertently say that I don't believe or trust the other person. We need to be open to communication, which is uncommon in Ghana. We need to be open to vulnerability - also not common in Ghana. Communicating openly and honestly is difficult and painful but also beautiful and wonderful all at the same time.

When two people commit to staying in the same room, facing their challenges, and working through them together, they will both thrive.

And thrive, we do!

I saved the money, got the visas and manifested for A.T. to be at a football showcase in Cairo in 2023, and now in Spain, hopefully to be signed soon. Together, we will manifest a football academy in the community. I can see it already!

With the help of my football agent mentor, John Viola, I will manifest my first professional player to be signed. And that is just the start.

Are you ready to manifest greatness in your life? Follow these three simple steps:
1. Believe in yourself and your cause. 100%.
2. See it, hear it, feel it, smell it, taste it, embody it.
3. Trust that all the pieces will fall into place.

I am a work in progress, too.

About the Author

Marie Schlemm is a mother, salsa lover, adventurer, sea swimmer, veterinarian-turned-chocolatier, educator, and now also a FIFA licensed football (soccer) agent. While many people start consuming chocolate while coping with trauma, Marie started creating chocolate! Working with chocolate combined her scientific brain and her hands while melting her heart along the way. She learned to love and live again through patience and surrender. In order to be a successful chocolatier, she needed to be in the present and let go of the pain of the past.

In 2022, Marie's fascination with chocolate and cacao eventually inspired her mission to help end child slavery in the cocoa industry. She invested in a cocoa farming community in Ghana, where there "happened to be" a team of young football players – many talented, all beautiful souls. Marie wanted to help them, so she started talking to scouts back in the UK and ended up sitting the FIFA exam for football agents in April 2023.

Now, her football network is growing and expanding rapidly, involving ex-world cup players, academies in Spain and Africa, and one of the longest-standing football agencies in the UK. This is just the beginning!

Chocolate and football will form one beautiful circle – spreading awareness and giving young people in cocoa farming communities not just hope but a real chance to manifest the future that so many only dream of.

Connect with Marie below:

- https://thetaoofchocolate.com
- https://www.facebook.com/thetaoofchocolate
- https://www.youtube.com/@thetaoofchocolate

REVEREND STACEY PIEDRAHITA

The Little Reverend Who Could

*"Manifesting is not about attracting what you want.
Manifesting is an awareness and an understanding that you attract what you are."*
~ Dr. Wayne Dyer

A*Reverend?* Come on, seriously. I never saw that one coming! This mind-blowing revelation didn't hit me until I was well into my fifties – lonely, disabled, and almost homeless.

2023 almost took me out. I was excited to jump back on the Law of Attraction bandwagon after Rhonda Byrne's book *The Secret* came out in 2006. I remember there was something magical about the concept back then. Looking back now, it wasn't until I put together more pieces, had a hell of a lot more life experiences, and became a Reiki Master that I understood the concept of energy healing and integrated that with manifesting, and finally, the Law of Attraction started to make sense.

I can see eighteen years ago, God started planting the first seed. Did The Secret change my life? No, not at the time. What it did do was blossom into something magnificent almost two decades later. Back then, I made the mistake of focusing on the wrong concept. Who wouldn't want to manifest the big house, the abundance of money, and the new car? Even though I succeeded and manifested all of this. All I had to do was keep my mouth shut and behave. That is almost impossible for a girl born with fire in her veins with a heart here to trailblaze, spread love, and raise hell. I am a magical, Manifesting Diva to my core, but it wasn't always like this.

On the outside looking in, I was the girl who had it all. I was pretty enough with a handsome successful husband and beautiful, healthy children. We had the mansion and the Mercedes, and I looked like I had it all, but I didn't. I never knew inner peace, and my heart was never happy. I spent my twenties, thirties, and forties with a broken heart that I believed would never heal until I was gifted with a very special visit in 2021 by an angel who rocked my world and completely changed the trajectory of my life after a crippling illness. Dr. Wayne Dyer was that angel (My Fairy Godfather), and he taught me that we manifest who we *are* – not what we want. His teachings

BECOMING THE MANIFESTING DIVA

changed my life. I recommend watching his videos and reading his books for anyone who wants to learn the truth about manifesting. Don't be surprised, though, if he starts to visit you too! He is sneaky like that! I can see now why he was brought into my life.

Please understand it has taken me three years to be able to write certain parts of my story and have the balls to come out with it. I have discovered that everything happens in divine timing. I waited a very long time to feel the sweet victory of living in God's love. Living every day, trying my best to walk closer to him. I will never go back to the old me. I have learned to love the shit out of that girl, though. What a hot mess I was. I promise if you call out to God in the deepest pits of Hell, He will rescue you and all of your messiness. You will get the chance to turn your mess into something beautiful.

Back to 2021. It was Spring, and life was good. I was working and feeling great. I spent one-weekend hiking, and the next morning, I woke up and couldn't walk to the bathroom without severe shortness of breath and chest pain. I was admitted to a cardiac hospital and spent eight days there. Not one doctor could tell me what was wrong. Every test and lab was normal. I was discharged on three heart medications. I just continued to decline over the next few weeks. I was requiring 24/7 care at this point. I was bedridden and could barely speak. I was prepared to die that evening because I was so tired of feeling awful. I let go and told God I was okay with leaving if it was his will.

Then something amazing happened: I woke up and was with God. I had a near-death experience. I woke up the next morning a different person. As scary as this sounds, it was the most magical night of my life. When I woke up the next morning, I shook my husband and told him, "God healed me." He thought I was nuts. I experienced a radical spontaneous remission from Lupus, Fibromyalgia, and Rheumatoid Arthritis as well. I immediately popped out of bed, and the shortness of breath was almost gone. My vital signs were normal for the first time in over two months. It was a miracle. Ten days later, I had surgery to remove my breast implants that were contributing to my debilitating symptoms.

The minute I woke up after explant surgery, I was able to take a deep breath for the first time in months. I instantly saw life with brand-new eyes. I spent the next ninety days recovering. I surrendered more to God. This is when the Archangelic angels, ancestors and spirits started visiting me. I was enjoying feeling alive for the first time in my life. Instead of questioning anything, I was open-minded, intrigued, and curious. Not once was I afraid. I trusted one day, this crazy world of mine would make sense. I spent those ninety days working incessantly on my spiritual and personal development. I distanced myself from everyone except my husband and a few friends. I just got lost in the magical life I was living. I made the most of my time while recovering. I started to embrace the art of meditation and mindfulness. I connected to the spirit world and lived in a very happy bubble.

Most people are very uncomfortable talking about God and the afterlife. Speaking and communicating with spirit was way too out there for me years ago. Now, I can't imagine life without them, and I wouldn't change a thing. Still, three years later, I call these magical interludes with my spirit team "Tea Parties in Heaven". I communicate constantly while they guide and protect me. I know it sounds delusional, but these moments bring such peace and joy to my life. I stopped giving a shit at fifty-five how this looks. It is a magical way to experience life. My advice is to embrace the unknown. Do not be afraid to change; seek your higher power with all your heart. Mine is God.

Religion was always foreign to me, even though I was raised Jewish for the first nine years of my life. Tragedy struck, and I started to run away from God. God was a completely foreign concept to me. I believed I was too damaged to love because of all of the abuse and abandonment issues from my childhood. I tried for the longest time to find God in church. I craved that feeling of unconditional love and inner peace. I am so grateful now that I didn't have a religious upbringing because shattering old, outdated religious beliefs sounds terrifying to me. I became a sponge, learning everything I could.

I think the transition to understanding I am a spirit living in human form was much easier because of Wayne's wisdom and guidance. I started the deep inner healing work. I was desperate for change, and I was ready. I started getting advice from Wayne more – half the time, I thought I was crazy – but I just trusted that one day everything would make sense. As a former nurse, the golden rule is: if you don't document it, it never happened. So, I documented everything. I couldn't get enough. I wrote everything down in my journals. I was in critical condition when I started hearing Wayne's voice. He is the one who planted the seed about becoming an author. Six months later On October 27th, 2021, It happened! I collaborated in a co-author book called; *Intuitive- Speaking Her Truth*. Within twenty- four hours, it became a best seller in eight countries and twenty-four categories. Another manifested miracle moment!

Before this, I was a former oncology nurse and nursing educator working at a job I loved. I never had a thought of becoming an author or a reverend, for that matter. I was deliriously happy. I knew there was something beyond my comprehension that I couldn't see. In addition, I kept seeing the number twenty- seven a hundred times a day. The Universe sends us daily signs. Do yourself a favor, and stop googling everything. Ask your spirit guides and invite them in. They will come in silence. You will start to hear the voices when you learn to silence your mind. If the voices make you feel good, lean into them and start listening. If they make you feel bad, ignore them. Tell them to get the fuck out of your head and start working on challenging those limiting beliefs. Let go of your EGO and surrender. Ask your guides what the numbers mean, and you will start having such serendipitous moments that you will not be able to deny their existence. I promise. Looking back, years ago, I had no clue that the messages were ultimately guiding me to my purpose. I started reading the Bible intentionally over the past year and a half. I am enjoying the stories, trusting my own interpretation, and asking my guides for guidance when I feel lost or confused. It was a great time in my life. I was building a Reiki business, doing book signings, teaching Zumba, and living my best life, or so I thought.

BECOMING THE MANIFESTING DIVA

Tragedy struck again in September 2022. We had just arrived at our Hip Camp to go camping for a few days at a farm with a petting zoo. I immediately ran up the hill to pet the animals. I placed my hands on the fence, not realizing it was electric. I instantly screamed and fell. In that moment, I knew something had drastically changed.

Since I was a nurse, I tried to manage my bizarre symptoms while the owner of the property kept insisting, I was fine. Despite what he said, my doctors disagreed and agreed this was the catalyst for my now dysfunctional nervous system and my body falling apart. Every day since has been a wild ride. I suffered significant memory loss and struggle with PTSD, ADHD and FND. Three disorders I have never had any issues with before the electric shock. I was forced to medically retire last year after not being able to maintain a job with all of my disabilities. It has been one medical disaster after another, with countless doctors and specialists not knowing what to do, moving forward just symptom management. All they do is throw new diagnoses and pills at me. I live in a constant state of "fight or flight", which is extremely draining and affects every part of my day. I am slowly learning to manage and come out of my depression. I remind myself every day it could be much worse. I am alive, and that alone is the most beautiful gift of all. My ultimate goal is to one day get off disability, but for now, I am just learning as I go and trying not to be so hard on myself. The silver lining is disability got approved. I have all the time in the world to continue writing and healing. Writing poetry and short stories has become my favorite thing to do besides camping and overlanding.

REVEREND STACEY PIEDRAHITA

I had to lose everything last year to see what truly matters in life. I am falling in love with the life I am living. I have learned that my words are like a wand. I am very cautious now about the energy I put out into the universe. Only love, light, positivity, with a little go-fuck-yourself. I refuse to put anything negative out into the universe or waste my energy on soul-suckers. You get what you give, so I am only giving good! I am moving forward with only positive intentions and inspired action.

It is true what they say: *Life is all about the journey, not the destination*, so if you focus on the journey, it will change your life. I do consider myself a manifesting diva after all I have been through and have survived. I truly believe the best is yet to come, and I can't wait to see where God is leading me. The path I am on now has led me to serve him in a way that nourishes my soul. Set the intention to manifest who you are meant to be. It has nothing to do with your bank account. It all comes down to how you loved, who you loved, and why you loved. There is no better gift. God will meet you exactly where you are. I have spent the last few years searching for the meaning in this life, and I found it after finding Me in the meaning after almost dying. I was never taught that God lives in us, and I believe if everyone searched for a God of their own understanding, the world would be a kinder, more loving, and harmonious place.

This shitshow of a world isn't what God wants. I was told this the night of my near-death experience. I was shown a world that is forever imprinted in my mind, heart, and soul. A world beyond all comprehension, Love, compassion, harmony, and inner peace for all.

BECOMING THE MANIFESTING DIVA

No pain, no suffering. We are all one. It completely changed my perception. Moving forward, *I will never fear death, because dying is what brought me back to life.*

It is up to us to find our own true North. I have been heading south most of my life. Paths change all the time. It is never too late to change your direction. Do not beat yourself up if you are a fifty-year-old fuck up. I promise you, God loves the fucked up ones the most. Learn to find peace exactly where you are and invite the Holy Spirit in. Life becomes a party after that. At the ripe young age of fifty-six, I find new joy in the simple things. I have a heart that is forever young, and a mind and soul addicted to spirit. I have a very intimate relationship with God. I still pinch myself, because I feel like I found the secret to life on the road less traveled. That is what makes my journey so magical.

> *Imagination is more important than knowledge.*
> *Imagination is the language of the soul.*
> *Pay attention to your imagination,*
> *and you will discover all you need to be fulfilled.*
> ~ Albert Einstein

Albert Einstein got it right! Imagination is key. I lived fifty-three years without God and my imagination. I lost my inner child when I was nine and didn't start intentionally healing her until my fifties. I spent five decades without her. Never again.

REVEREND STACEY PIEDRAHITA

Don't make the mistake I did, believing you need no one. I tried doing life without guidance from God. I will never make that mistake again. Do you want your happily ever after? God helps those who help themselves. It is up to you – and you alone – to get happy and create your own happiness. I find joy in the simplest things. Allow your imagination to take over. Start laughing again and have fun! When I started intentionally healing my inner child, my imagination soared. I started painting rocks, and my creative outlet helped with my symptoms, my anxiety, and my depression. Something so simple as painting a rock brought me such profound joy. I am still learning about myself every day. I know I am different. I am profoundly different now. I am at peace exactly where I am. Joy and happiness come from within. Go and get lost in nature, and God will find you, I promise. I was wrong about so many things because I was just too afraid to change, to surrender, and to accept the life God had planned for me. Once you have that connection to your higher power, no one can take it away from you. I can say with the utmost certainty. We are all God's children, and it is time we started acting like brothers and sisters. Figure out who the hell you are in this lifetime and find inner peace. Peace in you brings peace to others.

So, this is who I am now. Medically retired. Yet, at the core of my being, "my multiple diagnoses" no longer defines me. I am deliriously happy on a soulful level. I haven't manifested my mountain dream house (yet) or the secret to financial abundance, but

BECOMING THE MANIFESTING DIVA

I wouldn't trade my magical, manifested life for anything. I manifested myself!

Being disabled isn't so bad right now. I wake up every morning with profound peace and gratitude. I know it could be much worse. I spend countless hours with God. I am my own best friend. I am married to my soulmate. At any moment, I can have a tea party in Heaven. It is a spiritually blessed life after six years of following God like a little, lost puppy dog searching for inner peace. I am now following God's plan to continue down the road less traveled, and I am eager – but patient – to receive more manifested miracles. I see now that my beauty came out of my brokenness. My brokenness brought me to God. God brought me back to life, and I now get to dedicate the rest of my life to serving God in a way that revives and nourishes my soul through my writing and ministerial work.

I wished for a magically delicious life, and that is exactly what I got: disabilities and all. I believe God has a golden path for everyone. Some of us had to dig to China to find it, but I promise that if you seek it, you will find it. Just keep digging.

Inner peace is your birthright. You can't imagine – even in your wildest dreams – a life so beautiful. So, I call myself "the Little Reverend who could" because I made it up the mountain. I did it blindly, knowing that one day, I would have unwavering faith and taste the sweet freedom and victory of knowing God's unconditional love. I really can't think of anything sweeter than that.

So, where do I go from here? Who knows. All I know is this: I went into 2024 as the most adventurous, courageous, and boldest that I have ever been. There is a wild and carefree spirit about me now that I just love. Losing everything was just the beginning for me. This time, I am starting over from experience. I could find a million reasons to be angry at my circumstances. Instead, I find a million reasons to be grateful and continue to trust God and do good. Just like the little engine who could. My motto is: "I am The Little Reverend who just fucking did!" I will continue healing and manifesting my magical life until the good Lord tells me I am done.

So, do I believe in God and becoming a manifesting diva? Yes…and thank God I do!

About the Author

Reverend Stacey Piedrahita is a former nursing educator, reiki master, and inspirational speaker. After a debilitating accident in 2022 that left her disabled, she has spent the last couple of years adjusting to her disabilities, studying the gospel, and following her passion for writing while embracing her creative side.

Stacey has been an ordained interfaith minister with the Alliance of Divine Love since October 2023. After serving for more than thirty-seven years in healthcare, she knew it was time to set sail on an exciting new adventure in a way that nourishes her soul. She loves nothing more than teaching and being the bridge between religion and spirituality while watching the spark of God come to life in people's eyes.

Her darkest hours have been her greatest teachers. After surviving a lifetime of trauma, chronic illness, and self-sabotaging behaviors, she experienced firsthand the power of God's grace and mercy in her fifties. Stacey has walked down the holistic path of healing for the last five years and is passionate about lifting the stigma on mental health, chronic illness, and hidden disabilities while promoting self-love and empowerment while encouraging everyone to embrace their beautiful mess.

She is looking forward to building her heart healing ministry, The Chapel of Divine Love, which is devoted to teaching broken hearts to see God's divine light everywhere.

Stacey is a walking testimony to God's miraculous healing power – and our own. She is now ready to share her journey to becoming herself while helping others start living the life they were meant to live; she does this through stories, her magical connection with God, her unwavering faith, and her uncanny sense of humor.

Connect with Reverend Stacey below:

- https://www.instagram.com/revrocks27/
- https://www.facebook.com/rev.stacey.2024
- https://a.co/d/7kY2PFb

SUSANNE KURZ

Becoming the Manifesting Diva with the Handbrake On

Becoming the Manifesting Diva sounded intriguing to me right away. But did it call me? At first, I did not think so. After all, I had been testing this "manifesting" idea for a few years and had not really seen results. By "not really," I mean that there was nothing so clearly out of the norm that it could not have been just a coincidence. In short, I did not think that I qualified as a "manifesting diva" in any way. And there was yet another reason why I did not think that I would write a chapter in this book: I simply lacked the resources to invest.

Yet, you can clearly see this chapter here in the book. How did that happen? Well, in tune with the book's title, you could say that I manifested it.

Over time, I started flirting with the idea of being part of this book. After having experienced how powerfully and beneficially the connections that were created by my participation in the second *Evolving on Purpose* volume impacted my life, I wanted more of this magic.

Now, being an academic with a professional history in research and teaching at the university, I am inclined to be sceptical about "manifesting" and the "Law of Attraction" (LOA). These are esoteric concepts that are designed to be elusive since they are impossible to prove right or wrong (scientifically speaking). But they are also infinitely more attractive than the idea that we have to rely on luck and coincidences for a lot of things due to our very limited influence on external circumstances.

Despite my chronically sceptical approach, personal experience beats reasoning and proof for me every time, and I am always eager to learn and gain valuable experiences. Therefore, when I first learned about the concepts of "manifesting" and the LOA back in 2014, I decided to open up to these concepts and see where this would lead me.

The first step in this process was to look back and evaluate in this new light how things had worked out for me. I inspected two areas of my life: the one that had been a bumpy road, namely money and jobs, and the other that had been relatively smooth sailing, namely building and maintaining relationships. Here is what I found:

My best jobs have come to me with ease. Yes, I did take actions that eventually led to these jobs. But what I interpret as the ominous "inspired actions" that started each of these developments were not big or special in any way but rather agreeable moves I made because I felt like it. It seemed pleasant and rewarding at the time. None of them were directly targeted towards getting any of those jobs. In fact, those jobs were not even visible on my horizon at the time. The actions directly leading up to the jobs were rather effortless, too. I have put in a lot more effort to apply for jobs I did not get than the ones I actually got.

As for relationships, I had never been stressed out about developing them, not even when it was about a love interest. I simply did not feel needy, and I trusted that I would find my match with the right person at the right time, and even if it was not meant for me, I would be okay. Admittedly, I found my partner of over twenty years when I was still very young, so I never reached a stage of desperation after years of waiting and watching others be "luckier", but I got a taste of this desperate feeling during the years I longed to have a child. My love relationship, however, developed all by itself once I opened up to it.

That does not mean that I have never had difficult times in relationships, but I rarely feel needy. Whenever I do, it usually does not turn out well. This seems to fit the LOA and the teachings on "manifesting" rather well.

Now, let us take a look at some of my most fascinating experiences in more detail!

Most of my jobs in academia came to me with ease and little to no effort, but three in particular feel like true LOA manifestations. All three were interim professorships that come into being when a vacancy occurs, and someone has to do the job while the final successor to the position is being selected. In Germany, this usually is a lengthy process that can take twelve to eighteen months. An interim professor may also be needed when a full professor takes a break for a term with external funding, e.g. to focus on research. Both of these scenarios offered me surprising opportunities.

For me, these occurrences came totally unexpectedly: I had met up with a professor for a pleasant chat to connect and have a good time. In one instance, I also offered to teach a class in the following term if that was welcome, and in one instance, there was not even a meeting preceding the offer. All three times, I was asked if I was interested in acting as an interim professor without a single thought about it beforehand on my part, without my awareness that a vacancy was imminent, and without an idea that I was being considered.

These also were delightful experiences: There was a limited amount of actions that I had to take to get the contracts, the positions were estimable and relatively well-paid, and the work was enjoyable and, at times, even fun. I also had the opportunity to make use of my prior work, which reduced my workload. All these opportunities came along with perfect timing, just when I needed a job to make a living or to top up my savings and, in one case, at the right time to make it possible for us to find and buy my dream apartment.

During my time as a student and PhD candidate, I used to look at houses that reminded me of the one in which we had lived during the happiest years of my childhood. My parents had rented a large apartment in a newly built house in a village in the early 1980s. The apartment was on the first floor and had a large balcony where we could play and even set up a paddling pool or a little tent. Whenever I looked at houses built around the same time that had some similarity to my childhood home, I was always flooded with warm, cosy feelings. I imagined living with my partner in such a house in a similar neighbourhood, in a cosy, bright apartment with a beautiful view and parquet flooring covered with carpets, the sunlight shining through the windows, painting the rooms in a warm and soft light.

Well, guess what? Less than fifteen years later, we bought this apartment, where we are still living—and I did not even consciously notice at the time when we bought it that it had all the key elements! We even have a large balcony similar to that of my childhood. The only thing missing is underfloor heating, but I had not consciously envisioned that.

Now, let us do a little time jump and see what has happened in the past four years since I changed my professional environment completely. I cut myself off from any options to get miraculous academic job offers from my existing network, so most things have not worked out on the financial side.

Still, I had some experiences on a smaller scale that could be counted as manifestations based on the LOA. When I wanted to join Katie's second collaborative *Evolving on Purpose* volume but was unable to make the investment, Katie ran a prize draw just in time for me to participate and win a chapter. This led to interviews with two of my lovely co-authors on my Change! TV show on YouTube, which ended up not only with two beautiful new friendships but also with one of them giving me an idea for a new branch of my business to help fellow coaches, spiritual entrepreneurs, and healers with their technical stuff and content creation. I subsequently started to work with both of them. So, my participation in this book actually generated new sources of income for me! Meanwhile, I have won yet another chapter in one of Katie's prize draws: this one! Is there any more fitting way to join this book?

There have been more experiences that could be discussed here, like my breakthrough to channelling stories that led to my latest book and a new offer to channel personalised stories for others, some unexpected, seeming coincidences around my high fantasy TV series in development, and the speaker network that appeared in my world shortly after I had realised that I have a message now and that I want to network more actively. But the most stunning, miraculous recent occurrence was a financial win that can only be explained as a very odd coincidence - or as a manifestation based on the LOA.

In the summer of 2022, I had a few wonderful weeks. I will not go into the details, but I was the most relaxed in years. In this blissful state, while walking around on our balcony in the warmth of

BECOMING THE MANIFESTING DIVA

a summer evening, I thought that, right now, I would appreciate an influx of a specific amount of money with no idea where it could come from. I did not feel like I urgently *needed* this money. It would just make me much more comfortable.

Guess what? The next day, I received a notification from a platform where I had offered some fractions of Bitcoin for sale that someone had just purchased them for almost the exact amount of money that I had wished to receive. What was miraculous about that was that I had put these Bitcoin fractions up for sale months before for a price well over the market level. When someone accepted this offer, the market price was around one-quarter of my asking price. In other words, The buyer could have bought the same amount of Bitcoin fractions from another person on the same platform for around a quarter of my asking price but decided to buy them from me for almost four times the market price instead. So, I had an influx of almost the exact amount of money I had wished to receive right the day after I had made my wish!

At first, I did not believe my eyes. I logged onto the platform to see if the buyer had filed a request to reverse the transaction since I thought it must have been a mistake, but everything looked fine. The transaction was then completed and has never been revoked, nor have there been any scam attempts. To me, this is a miracle.

In summary, it was when I had an idea to do something that felt easy and pleasant but not special in any way (like connecting with someone without big expectations) that completely unforeseeable good things ensued. This seems to be my rather tricky flavour of "inspired actions": easy, incidental, and without any signs of the enormous effects they will have, hence completely unrecognisable in advance. And when I had a clear vision of what I wanted but neither urgently needed it nor thought much about how to get it, then it showed up - sometimes fast, sometimes with several years of delay.

With regard to income, even when I eventually received what I wanted, it usually did not come from one of the proverbial irons that I had in the fire in order to make it happen, but from a completely different direction that had little or nothing to do with my efforts. As far as I know, this is in harmony with the teachings about the working of the LOA, so let us say that non-attachment is one of the ingredients for manifestation to work for me.

Would I call myself a "manifesting diva" right now? Certainly not. But do I continue to learn and experiment and cultivate the connection to my inner compass that shows me those elusive, unrecognisable inspired actions that lead me to the good things in life? Most certainly. Therefore, my story and approach fit perfectly into this book as I am on my way to *Becoming the Manifesting Diva*—sometimes with the handbrake on.

About the Author

Dr. *Susanne Kurz* is a German scholar, creator, life coach, author and speaker.

She has worked for almost 20 years as a university researcher and teacher on the History of the Persianate Culture in Iran, Middle Asia and India before embarking on a new adventure.

In her "second life" as a coach and hypnotist, she has started to use trance states to "channel" parables and messages while also supporting clients who feel stuck and want to reconnect with their inner guidance or simply to feel calmer and happier where they are.

One thing that has never changed is her eager interest in people and their stories and her passion for breaking through limitations.

Based on several years of practical experience, she also offers coaching to actors on optimising IMDb, Wikipedia and social media and IMDb DFY services, now extended to show hosts (podcasts, OTT TV talk shows and YouTube shows).

Further services include video and photo editing, content repurposing and platform servicing (YouTube, Spotify, etc.) as well as book formatting and more.

Her most exciting project in the making is the high fantasy TV series *Magician's Blood* that combines her unique experiences and skills to form a vision for a brighter world embedded in the story of a gripping adventure with the *Vikings* star Ivan Kaye in the lead. Not to forget: Katie Carey will be part of the cast as well!

Connect with Susanne below:

- https://susannekurz-coaching.de/english/
- https://susanne-kurz.com/magicians-blood-series/
- https://www.facebook.com/SusanneKurz11

YANA WELLER

When You Ask, It Is Given

A six-year-old girl is looking me right in the eyes. She hypnotizes me with her deep, dark hazel eyes. She has very short hair, but you can tell it's a girl.

I have a knot in my throat, and I don't know why. Her eyes have a spark, but they are sad at the same time.

I turn the page.

There she is again – holding a medal and doing her best to smile at the camera. I can feel her awkwardness and insecurity standing on the podium.

"Look! What a wonderful picture of you with a medal!" I hear my grandpa's deep voice filled with pride as he pulls the Polaroid picture out and waves it in front of my face.

Here I am, staring at a picture of a little girl in a wet, oddly fitting bikini standing on the podium, looking into the horizon.

This September afternoon will change the way I feel about myself and who I am forever.

Tears roll down my cheeks and fall on the picture.

Why am I so FAT? This one question was the start of years of struggle, self-doubt, and self-hate. I avoided cameras at all costs. My childhood joy was gone.

My childhood was not filled with pink ribbons and silky dresses. I was shy, quiet, and lonely. After all, why would anyone want to be friends with a fat girl?

When I was ten, I hid a big jar of Nutella in my room. When I was alone, I would sit on my bed and scoop a big spoonful of Nutella at the speed of light. I would feel better at that moment, but once the Nutella was gone, I hated myself again.

When I was eleven, the USSR was falling apart, so my family decided to move to Belgium in Europe. I entered a big classroom, and the teacher was talking in a strange language that I didn't understand. It did not resemble anything I had ever heard before.

I sat alone, opened my brown and green notebook covered with yellow dots, and began to draw. First, I drew a picture of my best friend's house. Next, I drew a picture of me surrounded by friends. We were all dressed up, putting on Mum's make-up and laughing loudly. That was my dream then: to have some make-up to play with and a best friend.

BECOMING THE MANIFESTING DIVA

The school bell snapped me back into reality, and I watched as all the kids rushed outside to the playground. They screamed excitedly and pushed chairs out of the way as if no one could see me.

By the time I reached sixteen, I could speak seven languages. However, even though I had just won a math competition, I still hated attending school. I was never good at receiving love or compliments. I hated being seen, and my anxiety about public speaking prevented me from being heard.

But I kept hearing in my mind the voices of my mother and my grandmother, "Oh, you are fine," "It's not that big of a deal," and "Don't be dramatic!" My parents worked 24/7 and were out of the country most of the time. My friends would come over to study with me because I was good at explaining math, history, and physics. I was also very good at giving advice about love. The girls would come to me to complain and ruminate about their boyfriends and how unfair life is.

But even though I was my friends' "love expert," my own love life was practically non-existent. Instead of a boyfriend, I had "friends with benefits," which left me feeling worthless, unlovable, and never enough.

I returned to the one thing that could numb the pain and bring me joy: food. But I am a dreamer. I dreamt of possibilities. Every evening, I would sit in my bed and imagine living near the ocean by a beautiful golden beach, with a tanned and toned body, and laughing with the love of my life. I know one day I will be happy.

I graduated from high school and went to study law because that's what I had been conditioned to do for the last four years. I have to be a lawyer; that's what my parents expect from me.

I was petrified of the change. The school was crap, but at least I was used to it. Going to university, connecting with new kids, studying, and participating in all the social activities, I just wanted to be left alone. My fears were running – and ruining – my life. I was trying to sweep them under the rug and act like they were not there.

"Everything's fine. Nothing's wrong with me." I was in denial, avoiding my fears as much as I could. I would go to class and then back home—just like a turtle that puts his head in and out of his shell. I tried to protect myself by making myself smaller until I felt totally invisible. Rejection, loneliness, and anxiety were my constant companions, although I longed for true connection and understanding.

Nevertheless, I have always been a dreamer. Every night, while crying myself to sleep, I imagined myself as a successful businesswoman traveling the world, making an impact, and living my life to the fullest.

One day, while studying for my exams at the university library, I was so bored and frustrated that I did not know what to do with myself. I knew I had to do something else. I wanted to follow my dreams and live at the beach, but I was so scared of moving alone to a new country with a new mentality amongst new people – the same story all over again.

No way! I can't go through this hell again.

BECOMING THE MANIFESTING DIVA

My childhood trauma reared its ugly head again. Fear pinned me down. I froze as I'd usually do when scary thoughts would race through my mind, so I decided to decompress and read a book – not a law book, but a fun book. I went searching for something interesting at the university library.

I discovered Bard Spalding and his book *Life and Teaching of the Masters of the Far East*. I got so carried away by the book that I forgot I had an exam to prepare for.

Two years later, I woke up to a rainy November day. As I stared outside, everything suddenly clicked. I saw the fear that was running my life staring back at me through my reflection in the raindrop-covered window. A shiver ran through my body.

I'm alive. Making moves that scare me will also change me and give me the confidence to be the person I want to be. I just need to trust myself and listen to my inner being.

That same day, I bought a one-way plane ticket, packed a small suitcase, and left the following day. I was petrified. I had no clue where I was going or what my next steps were, but I knew this was the right decision for me. I had to break free from the fear, shame, and victim mentality that had held me hostage for all my life. Flying 6000 kilometers away from home seemed like the right thing to do.

I had only my suitcase, $800 in my pocket, and a big dream, but that was enough. You have to want it more than you fear it, and I did. Of course, there were struggles, tears, regrets, and lost opportunities, but I knew that the vision of the future I dreamed of when I was 16 awaited me. I had no idea how, but I knew it would all come true.

Some days, fear still got the best of me. I struggled to believe and hold on to hope. I just needed a hug and someone to tell me everything would be okay. But I'm a dreamer; I dream of possibilities.

In September 2018, while in the airport on one of my business trips, I came across a book called *Breaking the Habit of Being Yourself.* I read the entire book during my transatlantic flight, and suddenly, everything made sense.

It's as if lightning struck me: I live by the ocean. I've met the love of my life. I've built a successful executive career in the High-Tech industry, co-founded a health-tech startup, given birth to two amazing boys, and co-founded a Montessori school. The vision that I had when I was sixteen, it's all here today! I'm living it! I was so shocked and happy at this realisation.

I could not stop crying as I understood the unlimited power within me. This was a sign for me that the trauma, the challenges, the fears, and the limiting beliefs that I had been carrying with me through my childhood were just a part of the trap. I realized that the moment I trusted, surrendered, and went all in on my fears, the fears disappeared, making way for the magic waiting for me in my vortex. The universe aligned me with all the amazing desires and initiatives lined up for me. Everything I asked for was there, just waiting for me to let it in.

I realized that every vision I had of myself as a successful businesswoman traveling the world and making an impact in every

BECOMING THE MANIFESTING DIVA

detail was manifesting in my life. I'm being it, living it, and embodying it with every cell of my body and mind.

Twelve years later, I've been blessed to attend numerous retreats with Dr. Joe Dispenza, and I have become an advanced meditator. I have learned to accept – and even appreciate – all my flaws, traumas, and imperfections. I've been blessed to get a clear vision, to create a life that I love, and to pursue a successful business that is now impacting thousands of lives by being of service and helping women from over forty-seven countries heal from anxiety, improve the quality of their lives, and truly thrive.

I've been blessed to realize that opening the heart lies at the root of abundance and joy. Opening the heart is not people pleasing or walking over your desires. Opening the heart allows the unconditional true love for self to burn inside of you. This was a tricky one for me because while we are so good at giving love, it is extremely uncomfortable and awkward to receive and accept love.

I've been blessed to realize that self-love is not a spa appointment or a new Chanel bag; self-love is self-compassion. It is not feeling sorry for myself and making excuses. It's the ability to respect and accept myself, even if I fail, mess up, or make a wrong decision. It's the ability to stay true to myself and talk to myself as if I were talking to my best friend if she found herself in the same situation. Self-love is always having my own back.

When I was forty-two years old, my grandma gave me an album. I opened the album and was captivated by a picture of a little girl in a wet, oddly fitting bikini with a smile. She was humble, cute, and skinny. I hadn't seen that picture in thirty-six years. I realized how much suffering I brought to that little girl with innocent hazel eyes. And for a fraction of a minute, I felt guilty: guilty for the harm I caused myself in the past and guilty for not doing enough good for myself in the present.

Guilt is a destructive emotion that demands negativity and needs self-loathing to

live. But as soon as I realized that guilt was starting to take over, I shook my head as if to shake away every ounce of guilt. Instead, I opened my heart with so much love for this little girl standing at the podium holding a medal. Tears of love started rolling down my cheeks.

I love you. Now you are safe with me.

About the Author

Yana Weller is a dedicated wellness warrior, a functional medicine expert, and a brain health advocate. After a successful 15-year career as Vice President of Sales in a multinational hi-tech company, she transitioned to pursue her deepest calling - transforming lives through holistic health.

Yana has dedicated herself to focusing on the physiology of the brain and body as the foundation, specialising in the assessment and treatment of anxiety, depression, and other mental health conditions. She utilises evidence-based approaches, addressing brain imbalances at their root, emphasising the importance of nutrition, metabolic health, mental health and functional medicine principles to identify nutrient deficiencies and hormonal or gut microbiome imbalances.

Having empowered over a thousand women to reclaim their inner peace and self-confidence, Yana helps break the vicious cycle of anxiety by uncovering the root cause of symptoms rather than applying temporary fixes.

Her innovative Brain-Targeted Neuro-Nutrient Therapy delivers essential nutrients directly to the brain, enabling profound transformations. The unique treatment approach combining Brain Nutrient therapy and lifestyle change has resulted in many of her clients who had lost hope in their battle against conditions such as debilitating anxiety, depression, and ADHD seeing a significant turnaround in their lives without pharmaceuticals.

Trained by Dr. B.J. Fogg, the visionary founder of Stanford's Behaviour Design Lab, Dr. Fogg has provided Yana with a unique perspective. She seamlessly integrates his groundbreaking insights into her practice by combining Brain-Targeted Neuro-Nutrient Therapy with Stanford's science of Behaviour Design, which fosters emotional well-being and supports lasting habit change.

Yana believes in the critical role of diet in mental health. Research strongly links poor dietary choices to mood disorders, anxiety and depression and other neuropsychiatric conditions, highlighting the importance of nutrition in enhancing mental well-being. With her compassionate approach and expertise, Yana Weller is committed to empowering individuals to take control of their mental health and thrive.

https://pubmed.ncbi.nlm.nih.gov/31735529/

Yana's mission is to break the generational trauma that was passed to her grandmother, her mother and then to herself. She is here to break the chain by being there for her two boys, with an open heart and pure love. Yana is a mother, a wife, a friend and a passionate foodie. She loves her morning walks by the ocean, laughing, sharing, and hosting big family gatherings - her favourite nourishing moments.

Connect with Yana below:

- https://www.instagram.com/aid_anxiety/
- https://calendly.com/yannaweller/discovery-session

ABOUT SOULFUL VALLEY PUBLISHING

Katie Carey, created the Soulful Valley Publishing House in May 2021. International Best-Selling Author Katie hosts the Soulful Valley Podcast, ranking globally in the Top 1%. Katie uses both the podcast and the multi-author books as a platform to help metaphysical coaches, energy healers, authors, and creative business owners elevate their work so that the people they are here to serve can find them.

Formerly the founder of STAGES, an alternative mental health charity for seven years, Katie is an advocate for Mental Health and Emotional well-being, particularly since her health was affected when she was ill-health retired due to disabilities at the Age of 48, with conditions brought about by trauma and a lifetime of toxic relationships.

Katie loves blending science and spirituality and collaborates with people on the same wavelength in her multi-author books. Most authors have stories of synchronicities that led them to write books with Katie.

ABOUT SOULFUL VALLEY PUBLISHING

Katie aims to introduce these concepts and ideas to more people who are seeking ways to support their mental, spiritual, emotional, and physical well-being.

Katie has a history of working in TV, radio, and theatre as an actress and singer, which she manifested in her life in her teens. After 22 years of living in a Northamptonshire Village in the UK, Katie is returning to Rutland. She is a Mum to three adult children and "Nanny Katie" to her grandchildren. Katie has made it her life's work to educate people to find healthier solutions and break free from ancestral, toxic, and generational patterns of lack and trauma. Katie is passionate about raising consciousness and currently does this through her work as a mentor, coach, podcaster, author, and publisher, as well as through her songs and poetry.

If you would like to collaborate with Katie in one of her multi-author books or write your own solo book,

Connect with Katie below:

- https://pensight.com/x/soulfulvalley
- FB, Twitter, IG and LinkedIn @soulfulvalley
- Podcast: https://apple.co/3BkJdkn

BECOMING THE MANIFESTING DIVA

Katie's Amazon Author Profile:

More books, solo and co-authored by Katie Carey, are available on Amazon.

Published by Soulful Valley:

Soulful Poems: Heal the Heart and Soul

Evolving on Purpose: Mindful Ancestors Paving the Way for Future Generations

Entangled No More: Women Who Broke Free from Toxic Relationships Building Their Own Empires

Evolving on Purpose: Co-creating with the Divine

Soulful Poems: A Global Collaboration of Poetry to Help You to Heal and Grow

Other Publishers Books:

Intuitive: Knowing Her Truth

Soul Warrior: Accessing Realms Beyond the Veil

I'm So Glad You Left Me: 88 Stories of Courage, Self-Love and Personal Growth

Due to Release in late 2024:

Soulful Poems: Poetry to Activate Your Soul Mission

www.ingramcontent.com/pod-product-compliance
Lightning Source LLC
Chambersburg PA
CBHW061942070426
42450CB00007BA/1028